Rejoice, Beloved Woman!

The
Psalms
Revisioned

Rejoice,
Beloved Woman!

Barbara J. Monda

Sorin Books Notre Dame, Indiana

© 2004 by Barbara J. Monda

www.avemariapress.com

International Standard Book Number: 1-893732-80-0

Cover and text design by Rini Twait, Graphical Jazz, L.L.C.

Printed and bound in the United States of America.

Library of Congress Cataloging-in-Publication Data

Monda, Barbara J.
  Rejoice, beloved woman! : the Psalms revisioned / Barbara J. Monda.
      p. cm.
  Includes bibliographical references.
  ISBN 1-893732-80-0 (pbk.)
  1. Bible. O.T. Psalms—Paraphrases, English. 2. Women—Prayer-books and devotions—
English. I. Title.
BS1440.M57 2004
223'.205209—dc22
                                        2004006286

Table of Contents

Preface

If you want to learn about a rock, you must hold the rock.

If you want to know a person, you must hold the person.

If you want to know God, you must hold God.

In the Psalms we hold God and are held by God. We are taught and we learn. We are loved and we are transformed.

God is not gender bound yet the portrayal of God as male has created an imbalance that can only be truly known by the experience of a different view, the view of God the Mother.

These Psalms were written for women who for thousands of years have looked into mirrors and have not seen the image of God.

Shaddai has returned.

Let us honor her and ourselves.

Dedication

To
Sister Eleanor Gorman, O.S.U.,
who taught me to dig in the dirt and
plant pansies and petunias in
God's Little Half Acre
back behind the grape arbor.

Thank you
for that
and for so much more.

Acknowledgments

The search for spiritual authenticity can lead one in many directions. Native Americans have played a role in my search and I want to thank them for helping me realize the need for me to find my own heritage of women's Judeo-Christian spirituality.

I also want to thank courageous women writers and researchers who have dug this feminine spiritual heritage out of near oblivion. Their rediscovery and presentation of it back to the world has allowed for the inspiration and edification of both men and women and enabled the possibility of a balance and cooperation necessary for both genders to be whole.

Lastly I want to thank Sr. Margaret Kunze, O.S.B. (now deceased) for her editing of some of the manuscript, Srs. Mary Giles and Laura Swan, O.S.B., for their encouragement, and Karen Kahler Shannon, of Sorin Books, for her confidence in this work and skilled assistance in birthing it to life in such a joyful manner.

Introduction

In the Jewish and Christian heritage, the Psalms are the prayers of the people of God. They are the universally accepted prayers of ritual in the worship of religions based on the Bible. They are also the private prayers of each person spoken in personal hope of divine intercession for a variety of reasons. They are the official prayer of Catholic clergy and religious who, when the entire Holy Office is recited, do, in fact, recite all 150 psalms in one week's duration. The Psalms articulate the basis of the human person's yearning for God. *But the Psalms are prayers from a distinctly male perspective that has caused generations of women to feel excluded.* They speak for humanity in men's voices, using masculine images, appraising problems in masculine understanding, and portraying solutions to problems in a man's approach.

It is assumed that these prayers, in speaking for men, automatically speak for women. It is assumed that somewhere hidden in the language of *He* and *Lord* and *Master* there is a commonality with women. It is assumed that, like men, women appraise justice as the annihilation of an enemy and the establishment of the people of God *over* the enemy's lands and servants. There is no adjustment for feminine tasks or ways of relating, or for images of a feminine God, or even any notion that the Psalms themselves were written to represent women also. In Psalm 1, verse 1, the writer states: "Blessed is the man (woman) who walks not in the counsel of the wicked. . . ." This *mental* insertion of women into what is written for men, and by men, simply does not create the same bonding effect for women as something written specifically for them using their images.

In my re-writing of the Psalms for women, I have attempted to demonstrate the affinity women can have for the Psalms that has come to men automatically for thousands of years. In a perfect world God is genderless and all persons, regardless of sexual category, can relate to language used to inspire the soul to morally virtuous expression. We do not, however, live in this world yet, and I believe that before we can realize this ideal we must acknowledge that there is a gender imbalance present in society, and in scripture as well, that empowers men at the expense of women. *Rejoice, Beloved Woman!* offers to women the experience of having, among many other things, *God in her own image* and words that portray a female way of being that embodies strength and nurturing.

I have not translated the Psalms: I have rewritten them. I have, however, attempted to remain true to the theme of the psalmist in almost all of the psalms. I have also changed many approaches to the problems at hand and added introspection as another viable way of making changes in one's self as well as the world at large. I allow violence to stand in many instances since the psalms are written for real people and violence is a human condition. I have, of course, inserted feminine analogies, images, and names for God.

Catholic nuns, priests, and brothers, who were bound to pray the Psalms every day of their lives, were instructed that if they were not able to recite them aloud in choir or sing them in chant, they must mouth the words as they prayed them in private, since the Psalms are public prayers and are meant to be recited aloud. Spoken aloud they are common prayers for all God's people and power is experienced through their use. A woman reciting these psalms aloud will experience this as she has not before.

Women of all nationalities and faiths have experienced the marginalization of their lives and the devaluation of their contributions, socially, economically, and spiritually. *Rejoice, Beloved Woman!* can serve to remind women that they are the givers of life, the earth's caretakers, and intercessors between the spirit world and people. This has been so from the beginning of time and will remain true as long as there are humans on this earth. Ancient religions were goddess based before males began to testify to their *his-story*. Slowly goddesses became lost and gods replaced them. Women's names became omitted and then forgotten. Women's deeds were no longer recorded.

It is my hope that all women, in their recitation of these psalms, will feel a strengthening of their bond with other women and a stronger love of themselves as women because they can now experience the presence and power of God in their lives, in a way they have never done before—a God who reflects them and speaks in their language, and whose power is also their power.

Barbara J. Monda

Feminine Aspects of God in the Bible

Chokmah, or Hokmah, is the second of the ten sefirot in the biblical writings of the Kabbalah and the personification of divine wisdom, the element emerging from nothing. She is the point of beginning, a designated primordial origin before all else. She is the seed that preexists the plant. Chokmah represents God's plan of what might come into existence in the future. She is, therefore, the potentiality of all existence. Everything that is later to be found in the creation is found first in Chokmah. Instead of existing in phenomena, in Chokmah, all exists as concepts, ideas, or principles. She is the idea of what can be. The color associated with Chokmah is blue since she comes forth from the blackness of nothing. There is some dispute as to whether Chokmah is personified as male or female, but some interpretations argue for femaleness, as Chokmah's main attribute is wisdom.

Binah is the third of the ten sefirot in the Kabbalah and represents the stage when the raw energy of the intellect or wisdom of Chokmah finds form in mature womanhood. Thus, Binah is associated with the divine womb, the vehicle of wholeness. She brings potential into reality. She embodies the "god-ness" in creation. She becomes the unity of God and the world. As the divine mother and the mother of the Shekhinah, she is the world that is coming, constantly coming, and never stopping. Binah is also the definitive feminine element in the Godhead, symbolizing ultimate understanding and discernment. Having received the seed, Binah conceives and gives birth to everything. Since she is the mother of the Shekhinah, many of the symbols associated with Binah are, therefore, identical to those of the Shekhinah. The color associated with Binah is green.

Shekhinah, or the Shekhinah, is the last of the ten sefirot and a divine female entity. She is God's dwelling and immanence in the world with her people. Shekhinah is the bedrock, the earth, dry land, and the reflective quality of the moon. She is God the rainbow, coming wrapped in a cloud; the cosmic body of God's presence. Shekhinah is the kingdom containing all souls, the Sabbath queen, the God-bride of the God-groom. She embodies those aspects of God that are most closely connected to humanity, such as the longing of the lover for the beloved. Human conflict and the realities of life are present in her. She is, at the same time, the yearning for completion and the motivation and need for redemption. It is through the Shekhinah that humans can experience the divine-human connection that encompasses all forms of life and knowing. The colors associated with her are blue and black.

Shaddai, or El-Shaddai, is the almighty and big-breasted God taken from the translation of the Septuagint by Jewish scholars in 250 B.C. The Hebrew word *Shaddai* was translated to "all-sufficient," and as *shad* means "breast" in Hebrew, and "almighty" means "sufficient for all," this feminine name for God is used to display the nature of God as all-sufficient, all-nourishing, all-sustaining: a Mother who provides the bounty for the survival of all. Shaddai nurtures all creation and she is sufficient for all. She is the powerful Mother who protects her children with the fierceness of the bear. She is lavishly generous with those who are faithful to her. In the temple of Shaddai all grace is found. In her absence there is famine and the languishing of souls. This name for God is used in Genesis 17:1–2 (in connection with Abram) and in many other places in the Old Testament.

Ruach, or Ruah, is the ancient Hebrew word for "breath" and "spirit" found many places in the Old Testament. This name for God portrays God as the divine wind, the Holy Spirit, and the breath of life. Her power comes to revive and to renew as well as to sweep away. Ruach liberates her people, inspires prophets, and punishes the faithless. She brings creation out of chaos and also creates chaos when needed as she sweeps away the unnecessary. Ruach can be the gentle reminder of God's presence, she can give insight, or she can express retaliation for wrongs. She comes whispering condolences at night and comes again in the morning bringing death by storm. Ruach is the life of God dwelling in us, our inspiration and also our call to change. Ruach is referred to in Genesis 1:2, Isaiah 63, and other places, usually translated now as "spirit."

Sophia is the Greek word for "wisdom." She is wisdom in divine form. Thus, like Ruach, who personifies spirit or wind, Sophia is the God "personification" of what we now refer to as Wisdom. She was referred to as the wise bride of Solomon and Christians revere her as Holy Wisdom. Sophia is prevalent in the wisdom books of the Old Testament: the books of Proverbs, Job, Wisdom, and Sirach all focus deeply on this female aspect of God.

The Psalms

1

1 Happy are you who trust in the counsel of wise women. They guide you to a right heart.

2 You will delight in their words and you will see wonder in all things that image them.

3 In both night and day, there is light that gives vision and there is light that blinds. Be cautious of people who claim too much.

4 They may be thieves eager to steal attention and feast on the unsuspecting who have eagerly revealed themselves.

5 Filled, they go off and leave behind the empty shells of those too willing to be open, expecting more than an ordinary day offers.

6 The holy among you appear as any other. Their counsel, however, comes from truth aligned to all there is; they exaggerate nothing.

7 It is by the gift that the giver is known. See what you have when a woman leaves your presence; are you empty or connected to goodness?

8 A good woman tuned to herself speaks the truth and no more. She believes God made her in her own image, with no regrets.

9 Planted in the presence of these wise ones, you are like trees nourished by the fruit that falls on you and yet sheltered from a burning sun.

10 Of their bounty you benefit, yet there is no cost to you in their giving. A holy woman rooted in God creates harmony from noise.

2

1 Why are you in turmoil? Do you not know how loved you are? All of creation is yours and God watches over you. She will quiet your fears.

2 You are her child and she is your mother. She longs for you as the she-bear for her lost cub. She worries about you as a cow over a sick calf.

3 Go to her and find arms waiting to hold you and kisses for your forehead. She will warm you at her breast and feed you with her milk.

4 Her comfort gives you strength and you will know you are her daughter. You are created out of a love as powerful as she is.

5 She chooses the challenges of each day especially for you. She will guide you through them and you will prove your worth.

6 There is no need for you to make of yourself what you are not. Those who pretend only confuse themselves and others as well.

7 Years are wasted by this fraud, serving no good purpose. Give her credit for her choices and workings with you.

8 No need to fear failure or to judge yourself harshly. You are too severe and this accomplishes nothing.

9 Do not be shame-ridden for what is not yet learned. Shaddai loves what you do and watches you grow, day by day.

10 Rejoice, beloved woman! See with her eyes all that you have learned in your years and continue to have faith.
She will guide you back to your eternal home, fulfilled and complete when your day is done.

3

1 My enemies surround me and nothing I say is acceptable. I feel alone and rejected by my family and those I thought were friends.

2 How long must I endure those who do not understand me? The weight of their harshness drives me into myself and I feel depressed.

3 Why do you allow this, O God? Am I not your chosen one who has sacrificed to follow you? Redress these wrongs and give me back my place.

4 This loneliness creates a fog that closes in on me and I am forced to sit and wait, emptying myself in an endless flow of tears.

5 My rage does nothing to change my detractors. Only you can humiliate them. Show they are wrong and break their bones, if necessary, to save me.

6 Am I forced to find solace in the company of the cold-hearted, a task more challenging than growing fruit in the desert or finding beauty in trash?

7 I search for you and long to move freely along the way of a discerning daughter. Clear the path for me so I can make progress.

8 You have ways of teaching me, Mother. I trust that the merits of your lessons will become known to me, as you choose to reveal them.

9 I rest in this emptiness for now, opened by my tears and forced by my aloneness to focus on things I would not choose to, in better times.

10 Peace is the gift I ask for, so I may know myself, and learn to accept what is only yours to lay open before me.

4

1 When I was hard-pressed and owned by my fears you set me free. I thought you were gone but you heard my prayers.

2 I am ashamed I doubted your ways. I want to sing now because you did not abandon me when my pain made me weak and selfish.

3 Even though I am an old woman, the pains of my childhood still grab at me and bring my spirit low. In these moments, I am blind and full of rage.

4 I cannot see the good in anything and I am not open to hearing others. When friends depart, I feel abandoned and do not see how I have rejected them.

5 My wisdom comes and goes as the moon fades from view and appears again. You teach me that the constancy of love is real even when it is hidden.

6 I strive to be constant also, while accepting my rhythms as the variations that create my uniqueness.

7 In my deepest sorrow I soak my bed with tears and bang my fists in tantrums. I need consoling, Mother; do not run too far from me.

8 As I fight with the demons inside myself and hate my image reflected in others, you are there in the shadows, waiting for my rage to subside.

9 You bring the gift of wisdom in your lessons to me. With your help I value the womanliness that is my crown and my confusion.

10 Give me rest now, ever-loving, ever-patient Mother. You are the keeper of my spirit and source of my strength. I will trust in you.

5

1 Listen to my words, Binah, and consider my innermost thoughts. Heed my plea for help.

2 I offer sacrifices to you to claim your attention to my needs. Incense fills my room, lifting my requests to you.

3 I have been set by you in this place and now I need your help. Surely a request from your daughter is worthy of your great ability.

4 Why is life so hard when intentions are right? Why are results often so far askew? Correct the results of my efforts so I may rest.

5 You have made me partners with creatures who are innately true to themselves, while I struggle to achieve my own integrity.

6 Each morning my thoughts rise toward you. The warmth of the earth is generated by you and oceans move to your rhythm.

7 Through your love I can be safe and remain in your house. Know that I will honor you with my songs.

8 I return your love by offering kindness to all creatures and to the earth: Your holy body, the place of my birth.

9 Protect me with a shield of invisibility from those who would do me harm. Set the wolf and lioness before me.

10 Dance with me when the task is done and I have succeeded. Then hear me hum to you with the sounds of my peaceful sleeping.

6

1 Mother, do not rebuke me in your anger. Do not punish me in your wrath. Be gracious to me for I am languishing and fear I may die.

2 I am terrified at my ill health, and wonder how long I have to live. Look on me with compassion and relieve my infirmity.

3 If I die what use will I be? I cannot praise you, sing to you, or remember your deeds when I am buried in the ground.

4 Surely one who is free of pain is more valuable to be in your service than someone bent over and afraid of each day's events.

5 I want to be cheerful again and you can restore my joy. Be quick because my strength fails each day and my moans are growing louder.

6 It is true there are those more ill than I, but that gives no hope to me. My youth is fading and I want to use more years working.

7 Do not forsake me. I have been a faithful daughter who has served others with a smile even when the days were long.

8 This pain has worn me out and my pillow is wet with tears. Surely you will hear my prayer and give me a light body and a clear mind.

9 I will make amends to anyone I have hurt and pray for guidance to know my faults. I will set the record straight and be strong.

10 I will sing to you and tell others how you come to those who ask. Mother, your greatness shall be known in every home in this land.

7

1 I am great because I am rescued by you. The world pulls at me but you wrap me with your strength and I am safe.

2 People attack me and want to drag me down, to make me sad and useless. They say terrible things about me, injuring my spirit.

3 Mother, if I have done any of what they say, I deserve to be shunned and criticized. But I am ignorant of my faults.

4 My eyes are blinded by my skin, while I fear others can see into me. And I fear they know things about me that I do not.

5 Help your child to know her faults so she may recover from this attack, before she loses her dignity and makes matters worse.

6 If they wish me harm because of their jealousy, then deal with them swiftly, so I may be free of this anguish and return to peace.

7 It is only cowards and those who desire no good who talk behind my back. They attack when I am defenseless.

8 Their assaults have no good purpose. I could grow in resolve and build a courageous heart if they spoke openly and faced me with caring.

9 I will wear my dignity and persist because you are with me and will see to the proper end of this affair. I will be strong in your protection.

10 Speak to me with loving words and I will listen. If I have done wrong, you will teach me and then forgive your errant child.

8

1 Shekhinah, how glorious is this world that everywhere bears the mark of your touch! I sit among the mountains and I am in awe of your beauty.

2 Babies in their mother's arms remind me of how you care for and know our every need. We are safe in the cover of your clothes.

3 You hold at bay those who want to harm and take vengeance. Your steadfastness is all around us and your love makes our hearts jump.

4 When I look up to the moon I see you there. When I see the stars I know they are jewels worn by you, signaling your presence.

5 You have made us just less than yourself. You have given us the caretaking of all the earth and the creatures on it as our companions.

6 Birds sent by you sing to cheer my day. Fish swim at my feet and the fox and deer bring joy to my life.

7 The work of your fingers is everywhere my eyes turn. The sun warms us from above and the rocks hold us from below.

8 The rhythm of the oceans and the passing of the moon are all ours too, woven in us so we will be fruitful as you are.

9 Shekhinah, I feel the greatness of you in my bones. How can I properly thank you for all you have done for me?

10 My soul reflects your love and my heart holds what you have made. I will be the cup from which others may drink of you and we will all sing of your wonders.

9

1 I shall give praise to you, Chokmah, with my whole heart. I shall recount all your marvelous deeds.

2 I shall rejoice and exult in you, whose image is all around me. I will sing praises to your name.

3 When you preside as judge, I know your heart is true. You see the perils around me and you guide me to safety.

4 You are the Mother of all there is. Holy ones are yours, as well as those with closed hearts whose minds are dreaming evil deeds.

5 Danger walks beside me and wicked people linger nearby. Death can come without warning and misfortune can steal my joy.

6 All is set by your hand for the formation of each of us. Bitterness alone is not a good taste, but set with sweetness, makes a good dish.

7 There is no situation that cannot become the fabric of a good dress. It takes a skilled seamstress to use well what is at hand, for her own good.

8 "Be cautious," I say to myself. I can see these things on a clear day, but when the clouds hang low I am blind and need your light.

9 I will listen to the guides who offer me counsel and want to help me discern the rugged path through these thorns.

10 I trust the challenges you send to me, to help me become more nimble of spirit and better able to follow you, Mother, giver of wisdom.

10

1 Why do you stand so far away, Mother? Are you watching as those around us fall prey to vultures?

2 Our prisons are full. We are surrounded by the victims of evildoers. We are not all strong and some forget your name.

3 I am fortunate to be in this place with those who keep me true. In my weakness I too fall away and am lost for a time in confusion.

4 Wrongdoing is part of me and I have been guilty of hurting others. These are lessons for the honest of heart.

5 Greatness can often be measured by the depth of the fall, and we all have fallen. Some who fall far may rise even further.

6 Let me not judge any, because the storm may move here to tear down my home. And I may need everyone's help to rebuild.

7 Instead, I will reach out and take the hand of the temporarily blind. I will be their guide until you grant them vision again.

8 I will sit with the confused and the wounded, and hear their stories of hurt. I will hold them and my comfort will soothe their spirits.

9 I will speak kind words to those who act vile. I know their hearts have been broken; they are like abused children throwing rocks for protection.

10 I spill out my own evil deeds to you, Mother. I ask to be forgiven for what I have done to add pain in this world, so I can find peace.

11

1 In my God I take refuge. I flee like a bird to the mountains. Under the giant trees, I cry and wait for you.

2 I am so deeply hurt I cannot pretend any longer to be whole. No matter how hard I try, my tears are wearing away my weak fortifications.

3 Nature's rocks are sturdy and trees deeply rooted. What chance do I have in a storm, when my foundation is broken?

4 Every time I try to build, the boards fall in on me and I am left with nothing but a pile of rubble. I know people laugh at me.

5 It is unfair that I have been hurt and do not have as solid a house as my neighbors. I am left to cope with junk, while they have castles.

6 I am afraid and yet do not dare take down my walls to rebuild. Who will shield me from the view of the mocking?

7 Damaged as they are, my patches still hold off the vampires. Where is it that I can hide and never come forth?

8 You tell me I will be safe in your care, but I feel I cannot trust even the right-hearted, since they see my nakedness.

9 Come, my Mother, cover me over with darkness and seal the eyes of any viewer. Help me dismantle the remnants of my damaged innocence.

10 Set my hand in yours to rebuild a temple of our own making, crystal and yet strong, reflecting your beauty flowing into me.

12

1 Save me, Mother, for no one who is loyal remains. Good faith between people has vanished.

2 One person lies to the other; both talk with smooth words, but there is duplicity in their hearts.

3 They say with their tongues, they shall prevail. With words as their ally who can defeat them?

4 Wicked and deceitful people get attention. What is of little worth fills our newspapers and televisions.

5 Those who lie easily have many followers among the greedy. People desperate for help are easy prey for those making wild promises.

6 Come, wise Mother, hear the groans of the poor, plundered again and again to fill the pockets of the rich.

7 Where has honesty gone? Is there no one who will stand and speak the truth? And is anyone ready to hear it?

8 Who will sustain and protect the pure of heart while they speak courageously? Who will carry the truth of their words to others?

9 What is the point of having prophets if no one listens? What advantage are words if followers fail in courage and hide?

10 Mother, give us the eyes of a fox, so we can see in this darkness spread by deceivers. Give us the courage of the grizzly to hold our ground and protect the weak.

13

1 How long will you forsake me? How long will you hide your face from me?

2 How long must I suffer anguish in my soul and grief in my heart?

3 Look upon me, Mother, and answer me because this grief can hasten my death and end my chance for redress.

4 Some hear my cries and secretly rejoice at my suffering. Others hear my cries and do not care.

5 Still others are deafened by the noise of their own business and are so blind they would not see me if I died in front of them.

6 Where are you when I need someone who knows my pain and can soothe my tremors? Come and stay a while, hold me.

7 My life-fire struggles in the cold wind of winter and I am afraid of freezing. Give me some rest and warmth; revive my spirit.

8 The desert is filled with dangers and I am weak, leaning against thorns. My tears flow into the sand like a river.

9 Yet my tears are fruitful and I am grateful. Flowers surround and cheer me and I am filled with wonderful scents.

10 I trusted in your unfailing love and my heart swells with gratitude; I rejoice that I am brought to safety.

14

1 Only the fool says in her heart, "There is no God." She says everyone is depraved and there is no good in the world.

2 Many are unfaithful and corrupt. Evildoers rape the earth, steal from each other, and abuse their children.

3 They have no understanding, and no good sense. They devour the faithful and leave the ruinous remains of their appetites behind.

4 They go about their lives as if there are no penalties for their evil deeds. Do they not know God and her love for the world?

5 Chokmah looks on the whole human race and sees who acts wisely and who follows her ways. She is enraged by what she sees.

6 There will be serious warnings and everyone will feel her wrath. Heed the signs she sends to you and work to make a difference.

7 What will we do if there is no safe place to live, and if the air is not fit to breathe? Where will we go if greed kills the forests?

8 Find leaders the people will listen to because it is time to tighten our belts and think of the years to come.

9 Is no one willing to stop this insanity? Know, she will have her revenge and there will be no way to stop her.

10 One way or the other, she will be heard. She will save the world! It may be the humans that will perish if they do not heed her warnings.

15

1 Who will dwell in your house, O Mother? Who will go with you to the holy mountains?

2 It will be she who knows her heart and follows its truth; she who speaks no divisiveness and loves with no strings attached.

3 Come with me to the mountains, those of you who live with courage and perform deeds with a song in your hearts.

4 You keep your word even when your own needs and safety may be compromised. You show respect towards others regardless of what they do.

5 You honor my ways and deserve a place next to me. We, together, are mothers and live the truth of who we are.

6 My daughter is the woman who gives of what she has for the good of the needy and does not benefit from the gift.

7 She holds her tongue and acts only from her own resource of goodness. She is not goaded into revenge by evil.

8 She does not take advantage of the weak or the dull, but teaches them through her love of justice and her patient ways.

9 The hills come to her and she reflects their softness. In her smile, Mother, the wonder of your being is seen.

10 Her body is a temple of grace, giving life to those she touches. She, like you, Binah, is forever giving birth to all she loves.

16

1 Hide me, Mother. I have come to you to find safety. Keep me close because I am not much good without your help.

2 I have told everyone you are Shekhinah and that you take care of me. You have given me all I have.

3 I am so lucky to live in this place with women who love you as I do. Shekhinah cares for me and insures my continuation.

4 Simplicity guides me while others live their lives honoring money and worshipping themselves.

5 They follow crooked ways and set rocks in their own path. They cause themselves great sorrow and endless trouble.

6 You, Mother, cover me except when I am pleasured by my nakedness. You fill me from your breast until I am content.

7 My birthright is surely very great. I am privileged to be marked by you, as one of your own.

8 I am honored when you come to me with advice. At night, you impart wisdom to my innermost being.

9 With you at my side I will be cared for. My heart is glad and my spirit rejoices; my body rests unafraid.

10 You will show me the path of life and fullness of joy. Your right hand is filled with pleasures forevermore.

17

1 Mother, hear my prayer. Give ear to my cry. I am innocent yet no one hears my plea for justice.

2 I need a judgment in my behalf. You know I am a person of good character and I follow my heart.

3 You have watched me day and night. You know I am not prone to meanness and I am guided by your words.

4 I ask you to bend down and listen to me. Show your unfailing love for your daughter, who now needs sanctuary.

5 Protect me as the apple of your eye. Hide me in the cover of your wings from foes who gather around me.

6 My attackers have killed their own compassion and they are blinded by their pride. They press in on me, forcing me to the ground.

7 They are hungry lions wanting to eat me. Get up, Mother, and smash them. Save my life and toss them out of this world.

8 I will pray for the hungry and for hurt children. I will see to it that the needy are given money.

9 You have tested my heart and observed me endure. Do not fail me now, as I have suffered much and need your help.

10 Mother, my plea is just. May I see your smile and be given a vision of your intercession when I awake.

18

1 I love you, Binah! You are my rock, my cornerstone, my champion, and my home.

2 You are a tower of strength for me. You are the cave to which I go to find peace and safety.

3 I call on you and you surely protect me from all I fear. I praise you because you deserve praise.

4 I thought I would die and you came to my rescue. I was drowning in my fears and you heard me.

5 The anguish in my heart had me shaking to my very foundation, and I feared my legs would give out.

6 You came to help me like a dragon breathing fire and smoking with rage. Darkness enveloped all under you and thunder announced your coming.

7 Angels accompanied you. Lightening bolts blasted through my fears and the calmness of your water covered me.

8 You came to me because you delighted in me and my efforts to be truly whole.

9 No matter how great my fears are, you will help me overcome them. No matter how hopeless the situation seems, you will fight for me.

10 You have set me free, granted me victory, and anointed me as a chosen one. I will praise you forever, honored to be in your family.

19

1 Shekhinah, I look to the sky and see the reflection of your beauty. Your glory, set in the stars, speaks of the wonderful works of your hand.

2 As one day gives way to another and night moves into the embrace of day, wisdom is given with no words spoken.

3 All I need do is look up and see. The bridegroom, Sun, strides from his temple and moves to the embrace of dusk and his welcoming bride.

4 In the beauty of her darkness, the bride revives his soul and balance is again restored. He, all over again, is vital, eager to bring the next day.

5 I, like the sun, am renewed by my rest in you, Mother. The cycle of my life is daily revived and made fruitful in your darkness.

6 I am open to the teachings of Shekhinah. She satisfies all my needs and her lessons endure forever.

7 God makes each day's events vehicles of wisdom. Observing her manner gives joy to my heart and light to my eyes.

8 I am enraptured by your teaching and drawn to it like a bear to honey. My vitality comes in studying your creation.

9 Hold me from wrongdoing and keep me from being distracted by my compulsions. I do not want to miss your lessons.

10 May my words and my thoughts be always acceptable to you, Shekhinah. May you be the foundation rock upon which I am built.

20

1 May God always come to you in times of trouble, and may the name of the Mother be your source of strength.

2 May she remember every discomfort you bore with a smile, and every time you put another's need first.

3 May all your offerings be noticed and every gift you gave, counted. She will aid you quickly and with great might.

4 May she grant you your heart's desire and success in all your plans. Songs will be sung out loud to praise your victory.

5 May she grant every request you make to her. She receives the homage of her anointed ones.

6 She answers you from her throne and even sends her Amazons to reinforce your ranks. We stand surrounded, strengthened by their spirits.

7 Wealth of true value is the heart that glows with the warmth of compassion and hands that rush to soothe injury.

8 Some boast of big houses and expensive cars, but my only boast is having you willing to come to my aid.

9 You, Mother, are a great God. Those who are not so fortunate to know you fall over easily when challenged.

10 But I, with you at my side, rise up and stand tall because I know you will come when I need you.

21

1 A wise leader knows she cannot do everything alone. Neither does the credit of her good works belong only to her.

2 Mother of wisdom, you have seen into her heart and granted her desires. You have walked next to her and secured her position.

3 You have granted prosperity, health, and other blessings to all who trust in you. And they are unshaken in their commitment.

4 Like flowers cared for by a tireless gardener, they bloom in the nurturing of a leader who is true to our Mother's guidance.

5 Those who abide in the spiritual garden of the Mother God and follow her lessons know no wanting.

6 They are directed in the ways of a prosperity that gives life to others, instead of feeding off the weak, as the immoral do.

7 An attentive leader is one who is open to God's direction and sees others as voices of the Mother. She is called upon to learn endlessly.

8 Together, as a nation, they take from the dark nurturance of Chokmah all they require to grow in symbiotic harmony.

9 Even when fire burns away the useless, ashes preserve the ingredients for vigorous life. A wise woman sees that death in winter brings life in spring.

10 Everything is in your wise plan, Mother. Joyful winds blow through the garments of the daughters who hear you and sing your praises.

22

1 O God, why have you forsaken me? Why are you so far away? Hear my groans and hurry to help me.

2 I cry to you by day and you do not answer me. At night I cry, and you do not respond.

3 Our mothers in the past have trusted you, and you rescued them when they called for your help.

4 I am nothing, not regarded as a woman. I am scorned and jeered at by everyone, an outcast in my own town.

5 Everyone who knows this talks about me and I am ashamed to show my face, fearing those who judge me.

6 They say, "She has called upon the Mother for help, let her find it there." I look to you for help, for it was you who laid me at my mother's breast.

7 You have been with me since I came from the womb. Do not keep yourself distant from me. I need your help.

8 Raging bulls and ravenous lions surround me. My bones are weak and my heart melts inside me.

9 My throat is as dry as clay and my tongue sticks to my teeth. I am besieged by detractors, who like dogs, drag me through the dust.

10 They tie my hands and my feet. They strip me naked and divide up my clothes, gambling for my coat. My bones are exposed for their counting.

11 I ask for mercy and they laugh at me, gloating over my situation. But you, Shaddai, are not far from me. You are my strength. Hurry to help me.

12 Carry me away from these bulls. Save me from being gored by rapists. I will praise you in the homes of my sisters.

13 You will be honored for not turning your back on the persecuted. All your followers will be praised because you answered me.

14 You have not hidden your face from me and I will sing to you and make vows in the presence of my sisters.

15 You will hold the marginalized woman at your breasts and satisfy her. Her heart will overflow with joy.

16 All people will know they can turn to you, when abused by the intolerant. You shelter all manner of people in your garments.

17 You have not abandoned those suffering from prejudice and hate crimes. You have taken up their cause.

18 You give vindication to those already in the earth and they praise you for your acts. Those on their way to the grave will rest in your arms.

19 I will live for you, and my children will know of your love. All generations into the future will benefit from your justice.

20 Shaddai has spoken and shown her might by saving her daughters from the teeth of the self-righteous.

23

1 My Mother is my shepherd and I lack nothing. She lays me down in green grass and carries fresh water to me.

2 I can rest in her watchfulness while my soul is restored. She leads me along the path to wholeness.

3 Even when I feel lost in my own darkness, I do not give in to discouragement because I have her with me.

4 Your shepherd's crook and cloak give me comfort, Mother. You prepare a meal for me in full sight of those who are jealous of me.

5 You have bathed me and massaged my head with rich ointments. My cup, filled by you, flows over the brim.

6 Goodness and love surround me and will follow me forever. I will live in your house all the years of my life.

24

1 The earth and everything on it belongs to the Mother. All creatures are hers.

2 It was she who formed the land from the sea and made it stable for us to walk upon.

3 What woman can go up to the mountains and be with the Mother? Who can stand in her holy presence?

4 She who has done right and has a pure heart, she who is honest and has not spoken untruths of anyone, will go.

5 Such a daughter will receive the blessing of the Mother and be saved by her intercession.

6 Such is the heritage of those who follow her, of those who belong to the Mother of all.

7 Lift up your heads and open the doors of yourselves to Ruach. Welcome her breath into you.

8 Who is she, this God so glorious? She is Shekhinah, Chokmah, Sophia, and Ruach: our wise Mother and Amazon God.

9 Lift up your heads and open the doors of yourselves to Ruach. Welcome her breath into you.

10 Who is she, this God so glorious? She is Shekhinah, Chokmah, Sophia, and Ruach: our wise Mother and Amazon God.

25

1 To you, O Mother, I lift up my spirit. In you, God, I place my trust. Do not let me be shamed by those who want to humiliate me.

2 No one who hopes in you will be rejected. Those who abandon you will be confounded by their own loss.

3 Teach me your ways, Chokmah. Lead me along the path you have chosen. Help me say "Yes" to what you set before me.

4 There are so many ways I can fail. I am surrounded by those who will benefit from my failure. They set snares to catch me.

5 My fulfillment comes from being open to what you send. You have known what is good for me from the beginning of time.

6 Forget the errors of my youth and teach me self-compassion, as you continue to forgive my faults.

7 Turn toward me and be generous with your gifts, Mother and friend. Help me because I am lonely and suffering.

8 Lighten my heart and relieve my distresses. Hold me in the embrace of your forgiveness and protection.

9 You have called me to integrity and holiness. My soul rests in the shade of your love and your smile gives me courage.

10 You, Binah, are my hope. Make my troubles disappear and deliver my spirit from depression.

26

1 Mother, take up my cause and vindicate me because I have been true to my calling and trusted what you sent me without questioning.

2 I know you are testing me now and I accept it. You see my heart and my mind are ever true to your love and your way.

3 I will be faithful to you even when I am surrounded by those who want me to dismember justice and reject the faithful.

4 I am so uneasy in the company of vicious people. At meetings I hate to sit and listen to them. I fidget and long to leave.

5 I will come to your house, and in your presence, I will bathe myself in the waters of innocence and cleanse myself of evil odors.

6 I will sit with you, Shaddai, and sing a song to you. I will give thanks and tell of the glorious things you do.

7 O Mother, how I love living with you. This place is full of the wonders of your Spirit and I am filled by you.

8 Do not sweep me away with others who do not honor you, but rather lift me up and cover me with love.

9 It is in you that I will know my fullness of being and by your reflection I will see my image. I am made whole by your gift.

10 I will walk confidently at your side, held secure in your truth. I will praise you in the midst of my family.

27

1 Shaddai is my guide and deliverance. Whom shall I fear? She is the fortress of my life. In her cavern I am safe.

2 When the malicious ones attack me with lies, wanting to eat me alive, they will stumble over themselves, and fall on their faces.

3 Even if enemies gang up on me, I will not lose heart. If I am violently attacked, I will still trust in you, Mother.

4 One thing I ask of you is to live in your house all the days of my life. Let me always be able to look up at your beauty.

5 You are my shelter from storms. In your tent I hide, and in your cave find my strength.

6 Out of danger's reach I play and sing to you, Mother. As a beloved child pleases, so I will please you, Shaddai.

7 I look into the face of God and my heart knows your love. Do not turn away from me or be angry with me.

8 Do not abandon or desert me. If I am orphaned by my parents, I know you will take me to your breast.

9 Do not give up on me when I naively believe in wild promises and fail daily. Teach me the way to live.

10 I know I will be strong and brave when you nurture me beneath your garments. Hold me next to your warm body.

28

1 I call out to you who are my rock. Do not be deaf to my cry. Silence is no help and without you I am doomed.

2 I lift up my hands to you and plead for help. To the earth I turn to look for your protection.

3 Do not abandon me to the scoundrels who are sweet to my face but sneer at me in their hearts.

4 Reward them in the same manner. They deserve to eat of the dish that they serve to others.

5 They do not care to discern the ways of the Mother nor do they care to see the pain they cause others. May they suffer their just destiny.

6 Blessed be you, my Mother, who hears my need. You are the powerful protector in whom I entrust my heart.

7 When I hear you coming to help me, my heart fills with joy. Songs jump to my lips.

8 My strength comes from God, who wipes my tears and rubs me with the oil of her love.

9 Shelter your chosen ones, shower gifts upon those who belong to you. Hold them and carry them with you forever.

10 Shelter your chosen ones, shower gifts upon those who belong to you. Hold them and carry them with you forever.

29

1 Dress in your best clothes and come to praise the powerful Ruach, who made you. Honor her as her greatness deserves.

2 Bow down when she comes. Listen to her spirit moving around us and through us. Ruach is here!

3 She is the water: the massive seas and rivers. Her voice is heard in the thunder bringing the rain to us.·

4 Her words are powerful and filled with majesty. Her thunder and lightning can smash the cedar trees.

5 Her voice causes the sheep to give birth before their time. The young oxen run to their mothers in fear.

6 Her voice thunders, shaking the earth and bringing flames to the wilderness. Her body moves under our feet.

7 She is a great swirling wind twisting the oaks. Ruach can strip the forests bare and she can hold back the floods.

8 Her power is awesome and all who witness it stand and are in awe. They cry out "Glory be!"

9 Ruach moves about in the world she has made. We see her in the fury of her storms. We are in awe and cry out, "Glory be!"

10 Ruach, we praise you and the strength you have. Bless us with peace and safety in the midst of your manifestations.

30

1 I will praise you, Mother, because you have come to my rescue and saved me from those who maliciously enjoy my pain.

2 I cried out and you listened and healed me. You returned me from despair.

3 In my Mother's presence there is life and in her absence there is death. Her gifts fill my soul as her silence drains my strength.

4 When she says "Yes" to me the tears of grief I shed at night become tears of joy in the morning. Again, I am made confident.

5 With you at my side I am like a mountain, strong and persevering. You are my friend and confidant, my mentor and my reflection.

6 I am lonely and despairing when you turn away from me. Anguish fills my void and I feel the coldness of death around me.

7 What good comes from a despairing woman and how can I do any good if dead? If you abandon me, how can our commitment be honored?

8 Look at me and be generous. Come back and let us resume our relationship. There is much for you to teach me and I hope to learn it all.

9 You have turned my groans into songs and my body dances again. I will change my clothes, put on my best things.

10 With joy, I welcome you; my heart sings to have you back. I am forever grateful to be your friend.

31

1 In you, Shaddai, I have found safety. You cover me over and hold me. You listen as I speak to you.

2 You are my temple, my home, my cave, my fortress. You are a rock protecting me, your namesake.

3 Life is full of problems and I am not so strong. I need you to give me rest and direction. I am confident your hands will point the way.

4 In your wisdom you know the truth of my love and you despise those who lie. I will trust in you and dance at your coming.

5 I know you will never abandon me even when my friends find me tiresome. They are dismayed because I am so distressed.

6 My heart and body ache and my eyes are swollen with sorrow. Grief consumes my life and even my bones ache.

7 Neighbors turn away when they see me. It is as if I am dead and forgotten. Am I like old clothes to be discarded, or like a broken jar to be swept away?

8 Smile at me, Shaddai, save me from shame. Discipline those who want to humiliate me. Silence their lies and open their hearts.

9 You are the cave, our shelter from conspirators. Hide me in the layers of your clothes. Circle me with the protection of your love.

10 I was too quick to lose heart. Like a Mother, you came to defend and reassure me. I will be strong now that I know I can rely on you.

32

1 Happy is she whose errors are forgotten, whose misdeeds are forgiven.

2 A woman who looks into her heart and admits to herself her own lies sets herself on the path of wholeness.

3 While she hid this deceit inside and denied its existence, she was full of anxiety and very ill. She scowled endlessly and groaned often.

4 Day and night the truth weighed heavily on her. Her strength withered like lettuce in summer's heat.

5 When she broke the silence and admitted the fabrication she carried, guilt no longer held her prisoner.

6 She was drowning in her fears but now she is safe again. Truth has made her whole and she carries no more shame.

7 You, Mother, are my protector; you saved me from my own ruin. You enfold me and I am now able to sing songs of my freedom.

8 God says, "I shall teach you and guide you in the path you are to follow. I shall keep you under my eye and watch out for you."

9 She reminds us, "Do not act like a wild horse or a stubborn mule. They must be tamed with bridle and bit lest they hurt themselves or others."

10 Deceit brings only grief, while trusting the goodness of the Mother heals this pain. Love dwells peacefully in the truthful heart.

33

1 Shout for joy to the Mother of justice and compassion. Happiness flows from those with a right heart.

2 Sing a new song to our God, Chokmah. Play loud and joyful music on your instruments.

3 She has spoken and her word has power. The earth is the proof of her love and her justice.

4 She spoke and gave birth to the sky. She breathed and gave birth to the stars. She holds all the waters, above and below, in her womb.

5 All of creation stands in awe of her. She uttered words in love and everything in existence came to be.

6 Chokmah confounds the logical and the power hungry. The understanding of her works is to be found only in the heart.

7 The union of our truth with hers makes us her children and insures our inheritance. She knows the contents of everyone's soul.

8 War does not make a nation great, nor does brute force achieve anything. Only loving acts give relief and cause healing to happen.

9 Our spirits are lifted by her example. She has become our teacher and our Mother.

10 With every fiber of our being we trust in the lessons of Chokmah, our God. We know her love for us and we continually await her words.

34

1 I will always give praise to the Mother. Words of thanks will ever be on my lips. Those who are depressed will hear and be happy.

2 Come with me and let us rejoice because God sees into our hearts and saves us from the things we fear.

3 She does not abandon us. We are never out of her sight. She comes when we are in trouble and ask for her help.

4 She sends spirits to surround and protect those who love her. Rich are we who experience her favors.

5 Listen! Do you want a long and successful life? Then be truthful and do the right thing. Make peace with others.

6 God speaks inside you and she confronts your failings. She will hear a plea for help and show you the way to make changes.

7 Our Mother holds those with broken hearts closely to her. She heals their wounded spirits.

8 The faithful sister is called upon to suffer greatly. As she endures these trials, God watches over her and is aware of every tear.

9 The unholy scramble to flee from what they fear but in their hiding and denial only death is certain.

10 Fear kills those owned by it. Shekhinah saves the courageous who place their trust in her. They are shown the path of deliverance.

35

1 Confront those who confront me, Mother. Beat those who beat me. Get out your axe and shield and come to my defense.

2 Bring shame and disgrace to my enemies. May they depart in confusion, scattered like straw in the wind.

3 Mighty Mother, chase them into dark and scary places. They attacked me without reason and tried to trap me.

4 Snare them in their own traps and drive them into the pit they dug for me. May their destruction come suddenly.

5 I am so happy you have saved me. Even the marrow of my bones praises you for rescuing me from such villains.

6 Liars came forward to accuse me. These were the ones I helped and they repaid me with grief, leaving my spirit desolate.

7 When they were in need I sacrificed for them. I went hungry so that they could eat. Now I want to take back my gifts.

8 When they lost someone dear, I mourned with them, as if my own mother died, but when I needed compassion they laughed at me.

9 You have seen all of it, Mother. Do not let them have the final say. Bring those who gloat over my pain to disgrace.

10 My friends need to see me avenged so they can believe in justice. We will celebrate in your honor and praise your work.

36

1 Some people see no reason to honor truthfulness. The maliciousness carried in their hearts comes forth in their words.

2 They delude themselves into believing no one knows what is in their hearts. They feel proud and confident they will not be taken to task for their faults.

3 They ignore the urge to be honest and their daydreams are filled with scheming. They open their mouths and in place of good words come foul lies.

4 No dishonesty is too wrong for their consideration. The more they can get away with, the more smug they feel.

5 But as for you, Shaddai, your love is as vast as the skies. Your loyalty knows no bounds and your truth is as solid as the mountains.

6 Your justice suffuses all that is. You care for every person and every creature. How wonderful is your abiding love.

7 Your children are given milk at your breast. They feast on the abundance of your body.

8 They drink from the river of your low places. You are the fountain of life and the source of enlightenment by which we know things.

9 Hold close those who are your own. Shelter the sisters with honest hearts. Let them experience victory.

10 Keep me from being a doormat for the vicious and keep them at arm's length from me. Bury the liars together and make sure the grave is deep.

37

1 Do not be disturbed by liars or envious of them either. They will wilt and disappear like dead grass blown away by the wind.

2 Trust in the ways of Shaddai and continue being good. Security and peace will be yours and your heart's desires will be satisfied.

3 Commit yourself to the Mother and she will see to your wholeness. Your goodness will shine from you like the noonday sun.

4 Secure in God, you need not be irate over the success of the deceitful. Such raging only brings about your own ruin.

5 The wicked will get their just due. Those who are true to themselves and the Mother will endure.

6 The unpretentious will enjoy peace in their homes. God knows the desperate threats of the devious will amount to nothing.

7 The evil ones seem powerful but they shoot themselves by their own acts. It is better to live an honest life than be rich with the loot of bad deeds.

8 The blameless are assured their inheritance. They have nothing to be ashamed of. God continues to care for them.

9 The righteous are always generous, unlike those who take and never give. God will cut off the selfish and bless with abundance the generous.

10 We are held by Shaddai. She directs our steps and keeps us from falling. From youth through old age she will continue to nurture us.

11 Good intentions and generosity fill the lives of the faithful. They will live forever. Loving and just ways secure their place with God.

12 The malicious appear great as they inspire terror, flourishing for a while like trees in fertile soil, but wait and drought will come. They will disappear.

13 The forgiving who make peace with their sisters will persist, sheltered in the shadow of Shaddai.

38

1 Shaddai, you are a fearsome Mother. Do not be so hard on me. I feel the sting of your discipline.

2 I know I have done wrong and my body is paying the price. There is nothing in me that is healthy.

3 My bad deeds overwhelm me and I am unable to move under the burden of guilt. Humiliated and depressed I walk around miserable all day.

4 I am festering inside and out. The stench of what I have done follows me everywhere I go.

5 I am burning with fever and my health is ruined. I am a broken woman; crying and groaning rise from deep within me.

6 My friends now avoid me; only you can give me what I need. I am losing strength and my heart is pounding.

7 I have no words to defend myself. It is as if I am deaf and speechless. Please come to my aid, Shaddai, before I break down.

8 Save me from the humiliation of losing myself in front of others. I cannot find relief from this pain on my own.

9 I know I am guilty and I am suffering for what I have done. But why am I rejected, without chance of atonement?

10 Mother, do not abandon me and leave me in this condition. I need healing. Come and save me.

39

1 I said, I will restrain my tongue and not lash out. When the hateful confront me I will muzzle my mouth.

2 I keep silent but the rage inside me grows and my heart burns with fury. Finally, I hold back no longer and my thoughts ignite into words:

3 What is my life all about? This brief span of time does not seem to amount to anything. It is like a fart blown away in the wind.

4 Compared to you, I am insignificant: a mere shadow who accomplishes nothing. I shop and hoard, but for what?

5 Do not make a fool of me, God. I am tired of feeling like a useless ninny. Why do I worry about anything?

6 I will be quiet now. I know everything is your doing. Show some compassion for me because this desolation is exhausting.

7 Without you I have no purpose. Everything I do is wasted. Give me some hope and show me a reason for my life.

8 Moths consume what I love and nothing remains except my breath.

9 Hear me, Shaddai. Do not ignore my tears. Do not treat me like one who does not belong.

10 I have come to live with you, Shaddai. Scold me no more. I need some joy in my life before I give up and die.

40

1 Patiently, I waited for you, God, to hear my complaints. Finally, you heard me and pulled me out of the quicksand of my dilemma.

2 You gave me what I needed to be confident of my footing. I am grateful and others, who saw my faith, are in awe of you.

3 I am happy to be with you, Shaddai. The ways of arrogant and wily people do not interest me.

4 The wonder of what you do for me is beyond my counting. There are so many ways you show your love.

5 You drilled ears for me to hear, without demanding offerings in payment. Now, when you call the roll, I answer and am ready to serve.

6 Your desires are written on my heart and it is my wish to please you. I am outspoken when I speak of you.

7 I have not been silent about your goodness. I have told everyone about your caring.

8 Your maternal love protects me, Shaddai. When my troubles are more numerous than the hairs on my head, I call to you for courage.

9 When I am blind and overwhelmed by my failings I call, "Shaddai, rescue me." And you come!

10 When the malicious sneer and say to me, "Too bad for you!" I know your strength will be with me. Praise to you, Shaddai, all-giving Mother!

41

1 Blessed are those who help the poor. God will come to them when they have needs.

2 The Mother protects them and gives them lives filled with vitality. She is the source of their joy.

3 They will be secure in their homes, and, when they are sick...Binah will care for them and restore their health.

4 My neighbors visited me as I lay ill. They searched for bad news while wishing me well.

5 hey asked, "When will she die and be forgotten?" With no compassion they came and spoke the worst of me.

6 Even a friend I used to invite to dinner turned against me. She said I must be evil and deserving of my misfortune.

7 How I grieve at having my adversity broadcast to the world. How sad am I to be abandoned by friends.

8 Look upon me kindly Binah, and cure me. I will know then I am special to you.

9 Do not let my enemies outlive me. Reward my innocence; keep me for yourself and hold me close.

10 Honor to you, Binah, God of all faithful people. I praise you forever and ever.

42

1 As a deer thirsts for flowing streams so do I long for you, Shaddai. I thirst for a living God. When shall I see you?

2 When shall I see the beauty of your face? All day I am taunted with, "Where is your God?" Tears have been my only nourishment.

3 My heart is filled with grief as I remember the good days when I led the people in praising you, Mother.

4 Why is my spirit so low and why am I restless? I place my hope in the power of Shaddai. She will come.

5 In my great sadness I remember you. In years past, the battering of your white water did not harm me. I swam securely.

6 The deepening of my soul demands suffering, but how I wish it were not so. By almost dying we learn the joy of survival.

7 Each day I am tested and ordained to serve you. And each night you come to me to reassure me of your continuing love.

8 Your steady, dependable love was with me even when I did not feel it. But now I wonder: where are you?

9 I thought you were the earth under my feet. But I feel abandoned by you and shattered by my adversaries.

10 I know you, Shaddai, are my God. You will deliver me because you are my large-breasted and fiercely protective Mother.

43

1 Vindicate me, defend my causes, deliver me from the narrow-minded. I have become political and made your adversaries mine.

2 Rescue me from lying malicious accusers. You are my source of righteousness. Why have you forgotten me?

3 I'm bent in half by the pain of this situation. The insults of these bigots grind me down. I am surrounded by mediocrity.

4 Send me the knowledge I lack and give me the comfort of your holy dwelling. I will praise you there as in times past.

5 In your home I will play the harp for you. I will come to your table with great joy, and wonder why I was so disheartened.

6 In quiet moments I ask, why am I so forlorn, so churned up inside by this event? I know my God is with me and I will be rescued.

44

1 We have heard stories telling of the wonderful things you did in the old days. How you fought for the sisters.

2 No weapon or army could defeat your daughters. The uttering of your name alone had enough power to suffocate the vicious.

3 You are my Mother and my queen. Your wisdom, your love, and your beauty delighted others and won them over.

4 You took care of your own, rescued them, and reduced to piles of shame those who opposed them. Every day we remember these events.

5 So where are you now? Our bills are piling up and we have hardly enough to eat. Slick liars steal our retirement money.

6 We feel like sheep led to their slaughter. We have been betrayed for pennies and gotten nothing in return.

7 We are humiliated in front of our equals. They make jokes about us. We have become a buzzword for failure.

8 Disgrace is always on my mind. I blush at the thought of creditors and those who know the details of our shame.

9 We endure this and do not forget you, Chokmah, nor have we wavered from honesty and compassion. Yet, you abandon us in this dark time.

10 Wake up; do not sleep and ignore our misery. You can see into the deepest corners of our hearts; you know our pain.

11 We face a bloodbath, like cows led to slaughter, while the liars look on and gloat. Will you ignore this, as we fall into the dust?

12 If we do not survive, know we died true to you. But haven't we groveled long enough? Save us in the profusion of your love.

45

1 My heart overflows with love and I am lifted into ecstasy. Songs spill from me as if I am a skilled poet.

2 Your beauty, Shekhinah, is unmatched. The wonders of language are your gifts to me. You are queen of heaven and earth.

3 When you hear the call of justice, warrior queen, ride boldly to the aid of the poor. Splendor and power are your clothes.

4 You are the source of equity and fairness. You love right actions and hate wrongdoing.

5 More even than our sister Amazons, your actions are decisive in the cause of right. Evil ones cower at your feet, lose heart, and run away.

6 You bathe in fragrant oil. Myrrh and aloe give joyful scent to those near. Music fills your ears and princesses surround you.

7 Your consort takes his place at your side. He is clothed in gold but is blind to everything, save your beauty.

8 He renounces all he has just to please you. He will fill you with children and rejoice at your fruitfulness. Your daughters will proliferate.

9 He will bring young men to serve you; and he will make loud and joyful music to declare his devotion to you.

10 All people will praise you, Shekhinah. The truth of your goodness will be known, and women will find a new honor in your example.

46

1 My God is the cavern in which I hide when the ground under my feet slides away. She is my refuge and my helper.

2 Volcanoes slip into the sea, waters seethe and rage, mountains tremble, and the solid earth cracks. Yet, I am not afraid, protected in the stronghold of Binah.

3 She is a river of joy flowing through the city of the faithful. She is God with us and she will not be undone.

4 Countries rage, men murder each other, governments fall, evil moves through the land; but when Binah speaks even the earth hears.

5 She can stop wars and murderous deeds. She can destroy weapons and restore peace.

6 Come and see the wonders she does. She forces enemies to talk. She gives honor to the shamed. She makes the selfish share their wealth.

7 She makes the deaf listen and the callous cry. Like the rocks melting under volcanoes they melt under her power.

8 "Put an end to your fighting and know me as God! I rule over the earth and all obey my wishes!"

9 The God Binah is like the raging bear protecting her cubs from the murdering wolf. Her fury will not be restrained.

10 She is the queen of all that is. She is praised by her cosmic creation and exacts homage from her creatures.

47

1 Clap your hands and sing to God with great joy. She is the most awesome God, the great queen of the universe.

2 She rules the earth and those who live on it. She makes the laws and her providence awaits the kind-hearted and ruthless alike.

3 She chooses our inheritance for us, giving what is loved to some and what is deserved to others.

4 Seated on mountains, she is praised by the songs in your hearts and the music of your souls.

5 In the shadow of nighttime, she comes to teach the quiet ones who have room for her in their hearts.

6 The garrulous and those busy with distractions are slow to grasp her ways.

7 Own yourselves and she will have a place with you. It is not errors that drive her away but rather deceit that closes hearts to her.

8 Those who work day and night, but move nowhere, drown in their own sludge. All negativity is like mud that makes progress slow or impossible.

9 Those with open hearts seek the Mother's ways. And she flies to these children and carries them to mountaintops.

10 Believers and nonbelievers know the truth of Shaddai's ways. Those who do not follow are still in awe of her truth and power.

48

1 Our God, Shaddai, deserves praise in all the places on earth. She is a noble virgin bride, yet pregnant with all that is and is to be.

2 She is the snow-covered mountain, pure and lofty. Like the mountain, she is majestic in her beauty.

3 Resembling a woman in labor she trembles and thrusts forth children, while the awestruck tremble with her.

4 In the waters of her body she washes the newborn and with her wind blows life into them.

5 From the river of her breast she gives milk and from the garden of her body her children take nourishment.

6 She holds them in the warmth of her temple and they learn the meaning of worship.

7 Protected in her arms they grow and under her watchful eye they swim in the pool of her wisdom.

8 They are covered with kisses and sheltered in the protection of her clothes. Her body is the home given to them.

9 She carries them with her into maturity like the kangaroo. Her attention and love are always theirs.

10 And when the child has finished its days, the Great Mother Shaddai opens herself and takes her child into her warm darkness to rest.

49

1 Listen carefully, everyone: I have wisdom to give you. I can see into the heart and my ear is tuned to the truth.

2 My insight is in harmony with God's music. Rich and poor, simple and perplexed, pay attention!

3 Do not be afraid! Power and wealth cannot save us. No one is smart enough or rich enough to bribe or fool Providence.

4 We cannot buy our way to wholeness nor can we trick death. Wise and stupid alike die and leave their possessions to others.

5 Neither can we entirely control our progress toward goodness. What has been set before us is what we have to work with.

6 Trusting in the fairness of Chokmah is all we can do. She sees our efforts and our failures as no one else does.

7 Do not envy or judge the rich since you are not living behind their eyes nor can you read their souls.

8 The poor and the powerful all pass on together, naked and empty-handed. It is only the riches of the spirit that move with them.

9 How well have they loved? Have they honored truth? Have they used well what they were given? Were they humble?

10 Wise Mother, Chokmah, knows the gifts that were offered them and what now fills their souls. Only this wealth will win a place with her.

50

1 Binah, Mother of all creation, works in the world from sunrise to sunset. She shines out of her holy places resplendent with incomparable beauty.

2 She comes forth heralded by raging storms and lightning. She calls her people to her presence, gathering them close to her. She speaks to them:

3 "I have no need of your sacrifices. All the world is mine, the forest creatures and those grazing in grasses.

4 "All birds are known by me as is every small creature of the field. They are all my children.

5 "Hungry, I would not ask you for nourishment, for it is all mine. Your sacrifices I do not need either. Rather, keep your word to me.

6 "Ask me for help and when I give it to you, then praise me. Do not quote the law and then turn your back to me when I speak to you.

7 "For what purpose is knowledge of the law if you make friends with those who steal another's mates or possessions?

8 "My silence does not mean I approve if you are always finding fault with your family or if your words hurt your neighbor.

9 "I will confront you so you know how your acts indict you, lest in your self-satisfaction you withdraw even further from rightness.

10 "If I left you, what would you have? Thank me and honor my name. The ones who keep my ways I will save."

51

1 Mother, show me the compassion that your unconditional love for me demands. Forgive my failings.

2 Bathe me, as a mother washes her child who has strayed into mischief. Forgive me the deeds I have done, causing grief to myself and to others.

3 I carry confusion from my youth and I fail you and myself. You are right to be angry with me.

4 Inside my heart I search for my own truth, but I need your help. Teach me and give me wisdom in my innermost place.

5 Rub me with scented oil and lift my spirit. I am crushed by my wrongdoing but I can be glad again.

6 You have loved me and wiped away my sin, restored my joy and given me reason to hope. Your spirit fills me with song and light.

7 I will tell others of your compassion and urge them to invite you into their hearts. We are all children in need of the Mother's love.

8 My lips open to praise you, Mother, because you did not reject me when my spirit was shattered.

9 In my sorrow and guilt, the walls of my soul were torn away. Before you I laid myself as a broken offering.

10 You accepted me and repaired my heart. You helped me rebuild myself and delighted in the work we accomplished together.

52

1 We are in the midst of those who brag of the evil they inflict on the weak. Their tongues slice across marginalized people like a knife.

2 Hatred is their guide. Their plan is to destroy any person seen as different. They enjoy that their words injure beleaguered persons.

3 The speeches they give are filled with lies but delivered as if they come from God. Their smile betrays that they enjoy being evil.

4 They have no remorse for the pain they cause. Maliciousness and slander fall from them like rocks, crushing God's children.

5 In your name, Shaddai, they curse women out loud, while in their hearts, and with their friends, they secretly curse others also.

6 These evil ones work toward the exclusion from justice of all people who are different. Yet, what they gain is really their own death.

7 Come, Shaddai, and fling the bigots to the ground. Leave them homeless, with no rights, financially ruined, ostracized, and mortally wounded.

8 Let the pure of heart watch what you have done and feel strengthened. Show what happens to those greedy for wealth and control.

9 The poor and diverse are like loved trees planted in your home. The variations in your people are like flowers in your garden.

10 We trust in your love forever, Mother. We have seen what you have done and we know how much you love all your children.

53

1 Fools tell themselves there is no God. Their deceitfulness and wicked acts are loathsome. Not one of them does anything good.

2 God looks among these people to see if there are any who have wisdom and follow goodness. She cannot find a single one.

3 They are all hypocritical and malicious. They follow leaders filled with hatred and yet claim to obey your commands, Shekhinah.

4 Are they mad? Do these fanatics not listen to their hearts at all? They devour the children of God as one would eat bread.

5 A terror will come to them, the likes of which has never been seen. They will cringe as Shekhinah knocks them to pieces.

6 You will not save those who lie and do harm to the innocent. Everyone will see the shame they will endure.

7 Deliverance from the persecuted comes from the cave of the almighty Mother. She restores the rights of her children.

54

1 Save me, Shaddai. Listen to me call out your name. Come, with your power.

2 Hear my plea, God, and listen to what I need. The bigots surround me.

3 They refuse to hear truth, and reason has no place in their hearts. They are ruthless and want me dead.

4 You, Mother, will help me. You Shaddai, will come to save my life.

5 As for them, let their own hatred devour them. True to your word, Shaddai, wipe out these hypocrites.

6 Freely, and with gratitude, I will make offerings to you, Shaddai. It is right and just to give thanks to you.

7 You deliver me from every trouble and allow me to watch the destruction of those who want me dead.

55

1 Hear me, God. Do not ignore my cry for help.

2 Listen to me and come. I am terrorized by the power of my enemies. Their anger and hatred surround me.

3 They threaten me and I panic because of their rage. Trembling takes control of my body.

4 My heart beats wildly and I am afraid I will die. I feel shock at my impending fate.

5 If only I had wings, I would fly away and hide in the forest. I would find shelter from this horror.

6 Our town is full of strife. The predators are in schools and churches. In the marketplace they spew lies.

7 The weight of their oppression is felt everywhere. Their lies are believed by the guileless. Shaddai, confound their plans and silence them.

8 From hearts resolved to destroy come oily speeches filled with promises and lies using your name. Their words stab us like knives.

9 I can defend myself from an honest foe but this evil is not so obvious. This enemy is not so easy to see.

10 My own friends, people I knew well and confided in, are against me. I trusted these persons. They were my equals, my comrades.

11 I prayed with them and we took long walks together. They know my secrets.

12 Evil now fills their homes and grows next to them. Put terror into their hearts and bury them, Shaddai.

13 They have become a cancer to our town. They prey on all who come near.

14 Morning, noon, and night I plead for your help. My groans are my prayer to you. Save me, Shaddai.

15 I am human and I become overwhelmed and lose heart. I know truth and right are eternal and do not change.

16 You will hear me and strengthen my security. You will renew my courage in this battle I have undertaken for justice.

17 You, Shaddai, are eternal and have seen these evils repeated over the centuries. You know of their intention to oppress others.

18 I must trust in you, Shaddai; this is too great a battle for me. It is your task to save your children, to sustain the loving and faithful ones.

19 Toss the bloodthirsty liars, intent on evil, into a great pit. Do not allow them to grow old! My faith is in you, Shaddai.

56

1 Be gracious to me, Mother, I am trampled upon and oppressed. The days are long when foes attack.

2 I am harassed and plagued on many sides. Why is there such opposition to this just cause?

3 I trust in you, most powerful Mother. Your faithfulness to our covenant is my greatest protection.

4 They twist my words and wound me with them. They hide in shadows and plot to harm me.

5 I have to watch my every step and every word. The bigots cannot survive their own evil deeds.

6 You, Mother, keep a record of my tossing and turning, and you have gathered my tears in a jar to count. You keep a record of their deeds also.

7 No one made of flesh and bones can withstand your power. Maliciousness grows furiously in their midst and eventually it will consume them.

8 Our promises, made to each other, survive; I rely on you. When I need you, you come. No human can harm me.

9 I honor my vows to you. I offer gifts in your honor to thank you.

10 You revive my spirit and keep me safe. Your presence gives light and beauty in this life.

57

1 Take care of me, God. Watch out for me. In you alone I search for shelter until this storm is over. Hide me in the shadow of your wings.

2 I call to out to you, powerful Mother. We have a pact and there is work for me to do.

3 You, Shaddai, are my avenger who shames those who slander me. Cover me with your constant and true love.

4 I am forced to be with those who want to devour me. Like hungry lions their fangs tear my flesh. Their honed words pierce my heart.

5 Show your power over all creation, Mother. Let everyone see your greatness.

6 They tried to trap me when I was weak and discouraged, but their plan backfired. They fell into the very pit they dug for me.

7 My heart is steadied, Shaddai, my spirit calmed and resolute. I sing a chant to you.

8 I am refreshed and songs have returned to my heart. My life has been renewed, and morning is again a cause for joy.

9 I will be a drum and harp, praising you as I go about my life. Your love for me reaches into and beyond the clouds.

10 You are steady and sure and always present. Your love is bigger than the earth and sky. I praise you, Shaddai.

58

1 You who have made yourselves into gods, are your words true? Do you judge others with fairness?

2 In your hearts you have evil intentions. You cause violence among those who listen to you.

3 Your wicked ways were learned young. Shortly after birth you were taught to lie and your words have become as deadly as snake venom.

4 Your wicked nature cannot be charmed because you have closed your ears to the music of reason.

5 O God, smash the teeth of the wicked into their mouths and rip out the fangs of these lions who devour the innocent.

6 May they dry up like dead grass underfoot and may rains come and wash them away.

7 Let them dissolve into slime like a salted slug. Like a still-born infant, may they never see light.

8 Chokmah, mow down these thorn bushes before they grow out of control. And then, set them ablaze.

9 The right-hearted need to see this justice done. They will be washed clean by the tears of the evildoers.

10 People will know the truth and they will be assured there is a God who watches over the earth.

59

1 Shekhinah, rescue me from my enemies. Be a tower of safety for me. Shield me from those who pursue me.

2 Save me from evildoers thirsty for my blood. They wait to ambush me for no right reason. I have not provoked them.

3 I am innocent yet they rush to harm me. Wake up, Shekhinah, and watch with me. The malicious ones must be punished.

4 In the evening shadows they prowl like wild dogs bellowing evil words as sharp as arrows. They call for the innocent to convert to their ways.

5 You, Shekhinah, can laugh at them. You can mock them because you see into their hearts.

6 From behind your shield of love I can watch as you show yourself to them. The tower of your strength is my place of safety.

7 Catch them with the evil words stuck in their throats. Allow their own acts to incinerate them in shame until they are no longer.

8 False pride was their undoing. In your presence, Shekhinah, they were revealed and brought down by the power of your truth.

9 Yet there are other predators still with us. They come out in the darkness, scavenging for whomever they can feed off.

10 In these stressful times, I am happy knowing the strength of your presence is with me. You are a refuge where I can find unswerving love and safety.

60

1 Your truth, God, has broken down my defenses. I can feel your anger. I need you to restore me.

2 You have shaken up my world and torn it apart. Please repair it; I am falling to pieces.

3 You have given me great suffering. This bitter wine causes me to stagger in grief and I feel defeated.

4 I need a sign of hope, a place of safety. Reach out your hand to me and bring me home. This warrior is very tired.

5 You, Shekhinah, have power over all of me. Yet I feel divided up and parceled to divergent forces.

6 There are parts of me that do betray others and cause suffering. I know I can be my own downfall.

7 Do not let me destroy myself. Put your hand in mine so I know you have not rejected me.

8 My love and trust in you must extend to myself, or I will remain weak and a victim of my fears.

9 Humanity and womanliness are challenges and gifts from you to prove my vigor. Wholeness and strength come with the working.

10 Stand with me. Hold me tight enough to crush my fears. Renewed by your faith in me, I will again be filled with the love I must have for myself.

61

1 God, hear my cry. Listen to my pleading.

2 I feel far from you and my spirit is weak. Carry me to your mountain refuge.

3 You are my safety, my tower. You are my strength against foes.

4 Take me into your home and hide me in your arms. Protect me forever.

5 Hear the promises I make to you and give me the fulfillment of my wishes.

6 Give our country's just leaders a long life. May they dwell in your love and practice justice forever.

7 I will break out in song to you, Shaddai, powerful Mother, mountain of protection.

8 Each day and forever I will keep my promises to you.

62

1 For God alone do I wait in silence. She is my rock, my fortress, and my salvation. Success comes from her.

2 How long will aggressors attack and make threats? They hammer at their prey as if wanting to topple a wall.

3 Their goal is to destroy their opponent. Compliments may be heard but underlying them is hatred, revealing that their delight is in telling lies.

4 For God alone do I wait in silence. She is my only hope. She alone is my rock, my fortress, and my refuge where I am secure.

5 Shekhinah is my glory, my stronghold, my place of safety, my haven. Open yourselves to her and be held securely.

6 Some people are full of hot air, having no weight or substance. Tested, they dissolve like a mirage, like vapor on a hot road.

7 Do not be taken in by prideful sermons and promises of riches. They are the vehicles of delusions.

8 If you have wealth, remember it is not lasting. Steadfastness and substance come only with love and all real power belongs to God.

9 God's rewards come in equal measure to your wholeness and in light of what you do.

63

1 O God, you are the God I long for. My body yearns for you. My soul thirsts for you.

2 Like a dry and parched land, lifeless without water, so I look to you as an oasis. Your love is better than life itself.

3 Praise flows from my lips. I will bless you all my life. I lift up my hands and I call on you.

4 You are the great feast that satisfies me. I lie awake at night thinking of you and all you have given to me.

5 In the embrace of your arms, I sing for joy. My spirit clings to you, as your right hand holds me.

6 Those who wish me harm will die off and predators will feed on them. But those loved by you will be vindicated as you seal the mouths of liars.

64

1 O God, hear my anguished plea. Keep me safe from the terrors haunting me. Hide me from the scheming ones and their violent rages.

2 Their tongues are sharp like swords and their words are arrows aimed at the pure. Brazenly they ambush and shoot without fear.

3 They connive their plans in secret, trying to hide their evil plots, confident that no one discerns their hearts.

4 But they will be betrayed by their own words and Shaddai will shoot them down suddenly. They will fall in their tracks and be ruined.

5 Everyone will know what has taken place.
The right-hearted will rejoice in the sanctuary of Shaddai.

65

1 In the depths of my heart, I honor you, Shekhinah. It is there I make promises to you and you hear me.

2 All people are transparent to you. You know when they are burdened with the strain of life and you revive them.

3 Privileged are the ones with whom you share yourself. They are nourished by your bounty and find peace in your body.

4 I am awed by the generosity of your gifts, the beauty of the earth, and the vastness of the seas. You are hope and deliverance.

5 You have made the mountains and have wrapped yourself in rock. You can calm restless oceans and give peace to people in chaos.

6 We stand amazed by your manifestation. Even those not close to you are bound to marvel.

7 You are the Motherland, pregnant and bringing forth life. You nurse your creation with rain, which runs down deep furrows and fills the ocean.

8 You soak the hills, softening them to receive your grain, food for your children. All gifts come from you, Binah.

9 Every year is blessed with life brought forth by your touch. You bring lush riches to once barren places. The world is damp with your love.

10 Hills glow with happiness and meadows are made warm by sheep. Valleys, covered with grain, shout with joy and sing to you.

66

1 The earth, by its very existence, shouts your praises, Chokmah. All creation sings of your awesome deeds!

2 All confess your greatness; everyone is lowly in your presence. The cosmos sings a hymn to your name.

3 Come and see what Chokmah has made! Her amazing gifts for her people.

4 She creates a pathway through the river. Her people walked on dry land.

5 Her power surrounds us. We rejoice in her protection.

6 Her power lasts forever. She is watchful for the rise of the arrogant.

7 All creation, bless our Mother, Chokmah. She keeps us alive in her embrace.

8 You have tested, refined, and transformed us. Like silver, we are purified.

9 You have given us suffering, trapped us in our own prisons, and set burdensome guides over us. These are all ways of teaching us.

10 We passed through torrents and flames and received insight. Freedom is your gift.

11 I will keep the promises I made while being tested. I will return gifts to you.

12 You have held me, and saved me, Chokmah. I will use my mouth and my body to praise you.

13 Praise to the God who listened to my pleadings and did not reject me. Praise to the God who is constant in her love.

67

1 Be gracious to us, O God! Show us your smiling face!

2 The world will honor your ways. People will know your transforming, saving power.

3 All people will praise you. And you will accept the praise offered to you.

4 The whole world is joyful. You discern justice and work compassionately while teaching.

5 You champion equality and mentor all who care to follow you.

6 May you continue your nurturing of the world and be praised by every creature.

68

1 Shekhinah comes and her enemies scatter. They disappear before her like smoke.

2 Those with hard hearts melt like wax near a fire. Evil intentions cannot withstand her presence.

3 The just are glad; they rejoice and celebrate. Songs rise to Shekhinah, to her home in the clouds.

4 She is Mother to the motherless, consolation of widows, God at home with us!

5 To the desolate she gives her body. She leads the imprisoned to freedom and prosperity, while the stubborn are left in their own wilderness.

6 Shekhinah, when you call to your people, the earth shakes and torrents rain down. We know you are here!

7 You restore the promised heritage. You bring us to the expected place, refreshed and nourished.

8 Women hear your word and remain faithful to you. They are enlivened by your gifts and receive the prize of constancy.

9 Silver doves with golden wings are they, while the arrogant are scattered like feathers of a dead hawk.

10 Look up and find the beauty of Shekhinah in the highest mountains. No need to wish for more; she is with us forever.

11 Faithful and unfaithful alike behold her power. But those who are loyal receive her support and call her Mother.

12 Shekhinah is the source of our life and she is our joy in living. She carries our burden and feeds our enemies to dogs.

13 Your procession comes into view: young women striking drums and singing, "Bless Shekhinah, she is the fountain of vigor."

14 Children suckle at your breasts and receive life. Royalty follow behind bearing gifts for your temple.

15 Our marching steps and songs are filled with your strength, and we follow your lead.

16 Transform the bulls in government and on Wall Street, who in their lust for wealth trample the people. They sire calves thirsty for war.

17 Convert the warmongers and those sowing seeds of hatred. Even now their representatives come to you with offerings and prayers.

18 Make music to our God, Shekhinah, who rides on the clouds and speaks in a voice of thunder.

19 Recognize her power. She is home to the faithful and the bulls alike. Praise be to her.

20 Shekhinah, how awesome you are in your sanctuary! You give life and power to your people forever! Blessed be Shekhinah!

69

1 Save me, God! I am mired, sunk up to my neck. My feet have nothing solid beneath to hold me up and I see no end to it.

2 My throat is raw and my vision blurred from constant crying. I am exhausted looking for you, Shaddai.

3 My enemies are more numerous than the strands of my hair. They accuse me, want to destroy me without reason.

4 You know my failings, Shaddai. I do not want others to be disappointed or ashamed because of me and turn away from you.

5 It is for you I accept these insults and shame. I am an outcast in my own family, disowned by my brothers and sisters.

6 Insults meant for you now fall on me. My commitment to you is consuming all my strength.

7 I fast and I am mocked. I dress simply and I am ridiculed. Drunks and gossiping imbeciles make me the butt of their jokes.

8 Shaddai, hear my appeal. You can lift me out of this quicksand. Rescue my failing spirit before it is too late.

9 Do not let me be swallowed up in this torrent, lost in this cavern of hatred. Save me from being buried by these torments.

10 Shaddai, you are endless love, the source of all compassion. I am in need of saving; hurry, come and catch me.

11 You know the torments I accept and you also know the hearts of those who turned against me.

12 I looked to them for justice and found none. I looked for comfort and consolation and did not find that either. They have broken my heart.

13 I needed nourishment and from them I received poison. I thirsted and was given vinegar. Shaddai, make their eyes dim and cripple them.

14 In their security may their offerings be their own bait. May they be surrounded by their dead and deserted by any friends.

15 Those who torment the ill and ridicule their pain deserve to have their own misdeeds tallied. Erase their names from the ranks of the living.

16 I am suffering, Shaddai. Place your protecting arms around me. I will sing your name in songs and offer thanksgiving.

17 This will please you more than any bloody sacrifice. Praise and tribute are worth more than the taking of lives.

18 Be glad, faithful daughter, for having nothing opens your heart to Shaddai. She then can fill you with her gifts.

19 Your suffering is not ignored. Do not give up hope; you are always part of her family.

20 The earth and the seas praise Shaddai and all who are loyal will be her family. She will rebuild what has been destroyed and give it all to you.

70

1 Come quickly and save me, Shaddai. Shekhinah, hasten to help me.

2 Reveal the shame of those who plot against me. Humble those who wish my disgrace and ruination.

3 Let those who laugh and taunt me choke on their ridicule. But to those who search for you and trust in your love, grant joy.

4 They will sing, "Shaddai is our great Mother.

5 "She delivers me without delay. Shaddai is my protector."

71

1 In you, Shaddai, have I found shelter, you save me from shame. In your justice, you hear me and come to my rescue.

2 You are my rock, my fortress, a mountain of strength for me. You ordain me and deliver me from the vile.

3 You alone are my hope. Since my birth, I have depended on you.

4 You pulled me from my mother's womb and nourished me at her breast. You, Shaddai, I praise with all my existence.

5 Although I have become a target for many, you have wrapped me with protection. My heart belongs to you and I sing of your splendor.

6 Do not leave me now that I am growing old. Do not toss me aside as my strength fails.

7 My enemies continue to stalk me, forecasting my demise and threatening to overcome me. They attempt to convince me I am abandoned.

8 Do not be far from me, Shaddai. Their insults and shaming afflict my spirit and I am wounded.

9 Restore my hope in you. I will compose new songs of praise. My lips will tell of your inexhaustible acts of justice and redemption.

10 O Shaddai, I enter your temple and speak of your wonders. Now that I am old and gray you are still my refuge, my Mother.

11 I teach young women of your strength and power. You ride the clouds; no God compares to you.

12 Through misery and pain you raised me to higher levels of life. You taught me and restored my honor and then comforted me again.

13 I praise you with music, faithful Mother. My whole being, renewed by you, sings of your gifts to me.

72

1 O Chokmah, divine Wisdom, give your ordained ones good judgment and a passion for justice.

2 Teach our chosen leaders to be authentic and bring equity to the oppressed. Guard them from abusing their charges, or exploiting their power.

3 You give sustenance to the poor, safety to the needy, and protection from bigots. As long as the moon endures, you are with us.

4 You are like rain falling on freshly mowed grass, warm showers sustaining the earth. The innocent flourish in your care.

5 The seas and all rivers of the earth are yours, while those who carry hatred are lost in the desert, doomed to licking sand.

6 May all dominions honor you. May the patriarchal despots convert and come to serve you. The forgiveness they must beg for, may it be granted.

7 Chokmah will save the poor who have no one to speak for them. She will hear the ones no one cares for. Their lives are precious to her.

8 Out of their homes come blessings to Chokmah. More prized than gold are offerings of praise given by these glad hearts.

9 She will anoint and reward her daughters. Children will fill their wombs and their fields of grain will be as thick as forests.

10 The names of the chosen endure as long as the sun shines. The whole earth is filled with Chokmah's glory.

73

1 God is good to the pure of heart. She is faithful to the candid and intimate with the humble.

2 As for me, I nearly slipped away. I saw the riches of the wicked and I was envious of their success.

3 They seemed complete and satisfied, well fed and happy. They are well dressed and untouched by the burdens of others.

4 Their schemes to remain in power are slick and deceitful. Arrogance adorns them and violence is their robe.

5 Their velvety talk belies mockery and malice. Brazenly, they threaten to oppress others. Gullible people follow them and believe their words.

6 They challenge the wisdom of Chokmah. They boast that God is theirs and they own the world.

7 These deceivers are always at ease, surrounded by wealth while I am poor and full of anxiety.

8 Why have I kept my hands clean and my heart pure? All day I suffer and each morning arrives with new worries.

9 If I abandon my commitments and do as they do, I betray myself and become one of them.

10 It was hard for me to understand why I should be true until I was shown their destiny. Their deceit has made the ground under them slippery.

11 In a flash they can be caught and destroyed; everything taken from them. Their whole lives, gone like a dream.

12 I was stupid, allowing myself to be envious and bitter. I did not give way, however, and can now feel your hand in mine.

13 You hold me in your wisdom and preserve my dignity. Who do I have as constant and enduring a friend as you?

14 My humanity is weak and my heart can stray, but you, Chokmah, draw me back to yourself, always.

15 Wandering too far from you is dangerous. In you, Mother, I find all I require. Keep me in your heart forever.

74

1 Why, God, do you smoke with anger toward the ones you nurture? Why disown your own children?

2 This is the family you conceived long ago. You are our parent, our heritage, and our home.

3 The liars have left devastation behind them and have raged against you in your temple. They ravaged the forests and raped the earth.

4 They spoiled all they touched, burning everything to the ground. Your shrines and grottoes are destroyed and they tried to annihilate your people.

5 Where are you? How long will this last? Can you at least send someone to stop this?

6 Why be restrained in the sight of this? Why is your hand on your breast when you could kill these monsters and prepare them as food?

7 You create rivers and you dry them up. You establish the land, and make day and night. You give light to the moon and the sun.

8 The seasons come from you. You declared the boundary of the land. And now the enemy mocks you and ruins your creation.

9 Do not allow the dove to be fed to the vulture! Do not neglect your creation forever.

10 Remember, you have a covenant with us. In this time of darkness and violence, save the dejected who look to you for help.

75

1 Thank you, Shekhinah, for coming. We are compelled to retell the awesome story of your success in our lives. We hear your words:

2 "I decide when the time is right. I govern with fairness. When the earth is shaken and the people tremble, it is I who hold everything secure.

3 "I say to the overbearing, do not boast. I say to the malicious, do not raise up the hairs on your necks or think of goring anyone.

4 "Do not flex your muscles against me or mine. Do not speak arrogantly against my creation.

5 "There is no power in the East or the West, nor in the primeval places, that can produce a match for me."

6 Shekhinah alone is judge. She raises some up and levels others.

7 She breaks the bones of the evil ones and gathers up to her breast the blameless.

8 I will be true and praise Shekhinah forever. I will be true and praise Shekhinah forever.

76

1 She is revered in her land. The weapons of the patriarchs have been broken. No longer do they have protection!

2 You, Shekhinah, are radiant. Resplendent are you in the mountains of the bear.

3 The chief's bravest warriors are stripped of their ill-gotten riches. Numbed by your awesome power, they die frozen in fear.

4 Hearing your name terrorizes them and ends the destruction they cause. Their war is over.

5 You alone, Shekhinah, can accomplish this. The workings of tyrants enticed your wrath.

6 Who can withstand the anger of a such a Mother? You sent judgment from the sky. The earth was silent as all stood frozen in terror.

7 Shekhinah comes to rescue the victims of tyranny and to save the earth. The meek are vindicated.

8 Everyone knows you are the angered Mother who saves her children. Surviving despots now dance for you, Shekhinah.

9 Now, they pledge to honor your ways and recognize your awesome power. They will rebuild what they have destroyed.

10 They will honor the one who took the breath away from oppression. They will bring gifts to appease you, Shekhinah.

77

1 I cry out to God, hoping you will hear me. I am overwhelmed by today's afflictions.

2 I lift up my arms and plead to you, Mother, do not reject me. My soul is disturbed and cannot be comforted.

3 I long for you and grow weak from lack of sleep. I am troubled and brood on the memories of days long ago.

4 Can I ever please you again? Will you deny me always? Have you stopped loving me forever?

5 Is there an end to your promise? Can God be so involved in anger that compassion is shut off?

6 I remember your mighty works. I know the strength of your deeds and the power of your love.

7 Oceans churn and climax, birthing forth replicas of your love. The evidence of your promises surround me.

8 Winds blow, rain falls, clouds thunder and lightning sets the world aglow. Earth trembles and shakes at your direction.

9 Come, walk through my troubled heart, calm the rage in me and reestablish our pact.

10 Touch me and give me peace, Shekhinah. Lead me through these troubled waters as you made a path for Miriam and her people.

78

1 Daughters, bend your heads to hear my words. Listen carefully to what I say. Hear my teaching.

2 I will tell you stories handed down to us from long ago. The tales of ancient wisdom and the mysteries of our people will be yours.

3 We must not forget these stories. Generations to come must know of the glorious deeds of Shekhinah.

4 Every generation is in some way unfaithful. The teaching of the Mother must be shared and remembered.

5 The ancient women experienced the ways of the Mother. We now must make the effort to rediscover those ways.

6 Shekhinah rules the waters and they move by her command. She is the rock from which the streams flow.

7 Earth's bounty grows at her whim and disappears as quickly. We are fed by her will and she is nourishment for the next generation.

8 The sun lights the heavens and her words instruct us in justice. Our hearts glow in her presence.

9 Wind blows and we are moved by changes that come. Disoriented at first, we find security in her firmness beneath our feet.

10 Shattered by our enemies and filled with grief, she holds our hearts together and warms our shoulders.

11 Passing over the haughty, Shekhinah reaches to the child in us and holds up our innocence as an example to follow.

79

1 People pollute the world and destroy Shaddai's temple. They leave the body of God in ruins, while taking all they desire.

2 They kill women and children. There is no one left to bury them or to grieve. Animals feed on their dead flesh.

3 In fear and shame the innocent flee while rape and destruction continues. The cause of the honest working person seems lost.

4 For how long do we endure the slaughter? People are hacking each other to death for no good reason.

5 Who will defend the people in the battle against corrupt governments? Is there no one to come and help?

6 Our sensibilities demand a price be paid for the deaths of faithful people. Do not allow the predators to prevail.

7 Hear the groans of the unprotected. People who honored the sacredness of your temple are murdered.

8 Farmers, students, working people are slaughtered for greed. Nations are set against their own people.

9 Bosnia, Africa, Mexico, Iraq, Brazil, China, Palestine, Pakistan, all places of turmoil. Helplessly, outsiders watch the carnage.

10 May the wicked receive their due, seven times over. May good people be enfolded in your care, forever.

80

1 Hear us, Binah, Divine Mother. Lead your people like a mother with many children.

2 You, whose throne is in the sky, shine a light on us. Shake up your power and come to us.

3 Author of holiness, how long do you wait in moody silence? Your people need you.

4 Tears are our only nourishment while the enemy ridicules us. Restore to us what is ours.

5 You began something in Egypt. A vine was planted in soil you prepared. It grew throughout the land and spread across the seas.

6 Now, strangers steal the fruit and trample the roots. Why do you allow what you have planted and nurtured to be destroyed?

7 Return, Mother of all, and tend what you have begun. Cherish the fruit of your divine love.

8 May those who strike the faithful down, who slashed and burned the innocent, wither at your rebuke.

9 Rest your hand on the remaining faithful and give them strength. Give us the life we need to carry on.

10 Restore balance to this land. Your presence will renew us and we will praise your name.

81

1 Sing loudly to Shekhinah, our source of strength. Sing to the God of Miriam.

2 Lift your hearts to her. Play your music on tambourines, harp, and lyre for our Mother.

3 Blow your horns at the new moon. And blow again on the day of the full moon, the day of our feast.

4 It is a law for us, written in nature and decreed by our foremothers, to keep these observances.

5 Shekhinah, cosmic bride, wrapped in cloud, leads us to fulfillment. She is the manifestation of our future.

6 She lifts burdens from our shoulders. Delivers us from the evildoing of false gods.

7 "I am Shekhinah, source of all being, beginning and end of creation, Mother of all. From before your birth I knew you.

8 "Listen to my voice. Do not resist. Pursue your own ways and I will leave you to your own devices.

9 "If evil is your own doing, I will delay coming to your assistance. I will not save you from your enemies.

10 "Be faithful to me and I will come. I will feed you with the finest grains and satisfy your hunger with the milk and honey of my breast."

82

1 God presides over her creation and only she declares judgment. Her ways are not ours.

2 She allows the corrupt and the unjust to move about freely. The creation of our future is all part of this meld.

3 Shekhinah warns, "The lowly and the orphaned are your responsibility as are the oppressed and the destitute.

4 "The weak and the poor are the victims of your own violence. Yet, you continue to be ignorant and hide in the darkness of denial.

5 "The very earth is in jeopardy because of your stupidity. I have declared that you are gods. All of you are children of my body.

6 "But you will die as the rest have died. You will fall in your blindness.

7 "I, Shekhinah, display your conduct for all to see. Your own judgment is your due."

83

1 Do not be distant nor silent, O God. So many of your enemies are busy making plans against your people.

2 They plan to destroy entire nations, labeling indiscriminately those who fight back as terrorists.

3 Insatiable landowners form alliances with greedy politicians and businesspeople. They trap and kill off those you love.

4 Religious bigots and immoral developers all lend support to the demise of working people.

5 The land that working people look to for sustenance is taken from them. It is robbed of its ability to provide.

6 Come, Ruach, like a whirling wind pursue the voracious in your tempest. As a fire burns a forest, chase them with blazing passion.

7 Shame them, Ruach, into honoring your name. Humiliate them and force them to live in terror.

8 The earth is home and your people are caretakers of this world. We all are part of your sacred body.

9 Let it be known that God is all that is. She brings all into being and watches over what she has birthed.

84

1 How beautiful is your dwelling place, divine Mother. My soul longs for the garden of your temple.

2 My whole body swells with praise to the living God. How wonderful is your dwelling.

3 Gracious Mother, my home is your altar. Like a homing sparrow, or a swallow eager to nest, I fly home to you.

4 Happy are those who dwell in your temple. They will never cease to praise your name.

5 We are like pilgrims traveling through life's deserts. You fill the valley with cool fresh springs for us to renew our strength.

6 Life's battles give way to the inner struggles. And you, Divine Mother, show pilgrims the way to heal themselves.

7 Hear us, Shaddai, Mother of protection. See the faces of your anointed ones as they offer sacrifices to you.

8 One day spent in your court is more precious than thousands spent in the lands of the insincere.

9 Shaddai is the sun and the shade. To the blameless, she is all manner of gifts.

10 Blessed are all those who walk with her and learn to trust in her ways.

85

1 Mother, you loved the earth and restored the past fortunes of the innocent. You forgave the errors of your people.

2 You held your anger and calmed your rage. Now return to us for we are waiting.

3 Today we need reviving. Show us mercy and nourish our joy. Come and give us what we need.

4 I will listen to your words of peace. Peace for those who have changed their ways. Peace for the redeemed offender.

5 Peace for the generous millionaire. Peace for the honest politician, and peace for the protector of the forests.

6 Peace for the defending soldier. Peace for the caring leaders and the responsible citizen.

7 Love and faithfulness have met in you, Mother. Justice and peace have embraced in you.

8 Faithfulness appears from the earth and justice comes from Sophia. Everything convenes in the body of the Mother.

9 Shaddai's nourishment comes forth from every part of her. Fecund, the land springs to life.

10 Shaddai points the way. Follow her and receive the milk of life everlasting.

86

1 Hear me, Mother, and come to my assistance. I am poor and helpless.

2 You are my Mother, and I am loyal to you. Watch over me, save me, for I trust in you.

3 Fill my heart with joy, for it is to you, Mother, I raise my spirit. You, Shaddai, are good and loving.

4 You have constant love for those who summon you. Listen to my plea, Shaddai; hear my cry for help.

5 There is no one like you; no deeds compare to yours. You have made all nations.

6 You are great, Shaddai. Your works are wonderful. You alone are the Mother of all that is.

7 Teach me your ways, Shaddai, so I may walk single-mindedly with you alone. I will praise you with all my heart.

8 I will glorify your name forever. You have rescued me from the brink of despair.

9 The haughty rise up against me, and brutal gangs try to take my life. They do not care for your ways.

10 Rescue your daughter. Show me a sign of your love to frustrate my enemies and bring me help and comfort.

87

1 On the holy mountain sits the city of Shekhinah.

2 Her portals are the entryways to the most beloved dwellings.

3 Wonderful things are said of the land of our Mother.

4 The desert in spring, mountains covered in fresh snow, sparkling cities at night, all call to mind the glory of the Mother.

5 There is nowhere she is not. We name our birthplace and she is there. We travel to visit a friend and she is there too.

6 Authors, dancers, tradesmen, and philosophers all claim her as the source of their spark.

7 Everything claims her as wellspring and all are claimed by her as lineage.

88

1 At night, when I cry out to you, O God, let my prayer rise into your presence.

2 Incline your ear to hear my pleas. My soul is full of sadness and I am in danger.

3 Sorrow pulls me into the pit of death. I am hopeless and abandoned by all friends. They have given up on me.

4 I am in my tomb isolated from everyone and cut off from your healing touch. I cannot find your hand.

5 You have sent me into the deep. In the darkness of the cavern a shroud covers me and I am lost.

6 Shunned and disgraced, I live an endless cycle of pain. Humiliated and blinded by my tears, I cannot see beyond myself.

7 I cry out to you each morning, Mother. I raise my arms to you, imploringly. Why reject me?

8 Are not your promises kept in the dark as well as the light? The dying need your love more than the healthy.

9 My cries reach you in the morning. Show your face and do not turn away.

10 I have carried pain since childhood. Terrors and numbness have been given to me.

11 Rage has swept over me. I have been consumed by compulsions; surges grip my soul, tossing me against walls.

12 You have stripped away all my support. Friends are gone and darkness is my only companion.

89

1 I will sing of your love, Mother, forever and ever. Your faithfulness and love outlast everything.

2 God has made a compact with the descendants of Eve. Eve's children have come from Binah, the divine womb and Mother of all.

3 Her love is as enduring as the mountains. Life comes forth from her body and clings to her breasts.

4 There is nothing to compare to her. The heavens sing of her everlasting love.

5 She scatters those who do evil. Only she can call righteousness her own. Binah's touch can heal or it can slay.

6 Blessed are those who know her warmth. She is the essence of their soul and life is theirs forever.

7 Like a firstborn, ever anchored to you, Binah, we are loved like no other. Our antagonists also become your enemies.

8 Binah did not lie to Eve. All children belong to her forever. She is a Mother who endures the flaws of her children.

9 No one fully grasps the passionate depth of her love. Binah embodies all that is.

10 She has clothed us by birth and anointed us in pain. Her glory surrounds her. Blessed be Binah forever.

90

1 Mother, you have been our sanctuary. Before the earth and the cosmos were born, you were God.

2 You renew everything and everyone. Thousands of years are like one day for you. Life shoots up in the morning and withers at night.

3 Your power can sweep us away. Torn from all and laid naked we call to you.

4 Our souls are transparent to your glance. Our future can vanish like breath.

5 Our life may be seventy or eighty years long, toil and distress our companions. Then, without warning, our thread breaks and we are gone.

6 How long before you come, Shaddai? Console your child and warm her with the sun of your love.

7 Gladden our days; lift away our afflictions. Balance our sorrow with joy.

8 Show us the splendor of your accomplishments. Let our children, friends, and lovers bathe in your generosity.

9 Shaddai, your loveliness wraps us. You caressed our hands, and our labor is filled with your grace.

91

1 Remember, you live in the garments of the Mother. You find shelter in her shadow. She is the fortress, in whom you take refuge.

2 She frees you from the hunter's traps and saves you from diseases. She covers you with her wings like a mother bird shelters her chick.

3 Night terrors will pass over you and the evil acts of the day will miss you. Germs that strike in heat will take down others but not you.

4 Thousands may fall but you will be untouched. You will see the wicked chastised while you are held safe in her embrace.

5 Open your eyes and see how the iniquitous are repaid. But you have a large breasted mother protecting you.

6 Enfolded in her wings, Shaddai gives sanctuary to her children. No harm can touch them, no damage can come to their homes.

7 They will be carried and held safe from stumbling. Snakes and bears, wild cats and even buffalo will make a clear path for them.

8 Shaddai has promised, "Those who love me and abide in my ways are held firmly. I hear them when they call my name.

9 "I answer the calls and stand between them and trouble. I rescue my children and favor them with long life.

10 "To them, I show my sacred places, as well as the power I will use to save them. I am their salvation."

92

1 It is good to give thanks to Shaddai, to sing songs of blessing to you, great Mother.

2 At dawn we sing of your love for us and at night we sing again of your faithfulness.

3 Music of the harp, flute, and stringed instruments carry the melodies of our hearts to you.

4 We are awed to behold the grandeur of your undertaking. It fills us with joy to observe how potent your thoughts are.

5 The stupid ones do not understand that corrupt people, although plentiful as grass, are still doomed.

6 You, Shaddai, are eternal and you abide forever. The way of the virtuous will persist.

7 Come, watch the liars perish in their own deceit. Watch them attack each other.

8 With my own eyes I watch the self-destruction of my foes. As for me, I am anointed with fine oil and become as strong as a wild ox.

9 The upright are transplanted and nourished in the house of the Mother. They grow and flourish like the cedar of Lebanon.

10 They are full of sap, producing fruit into old age, eager to praise Shaddai as the cornerstone of justice.

93

1 Shekhinah reigns, clothed in glory! Shekhinah is girded with strength.

2 The world is created and stands firm in her protection. Her throne is established and will last forever.

3 The oceans pounding waves raise their voices to her. The seas shout, Shekhinah!

4 She is louder than the thunderous noise of the mightiest waters. She is stronger than the highest breakers.

5 Shekhinah rules from before the dawn of the universe. Those who are one with her praise her eternally in all her creation.

94

1 God of vengeance, angry Mother, show yourself! Rise up and judge the hypocrites in this land.

2 Repay the arrogant ones with what they deserve. How long will these violent gangs of politicians be triumphant?

3 Insolence pours from their lips as their speech betrays their true purpose. They crush average people and oppress those precious to you.

4 They have no care for the elderly, or for children. They murder the homeless and attack anyone who is not in their gang.

5 They say, "God is on our side and desires what we want!" I say, "Wake up, idiots! When will you fools catch on?"

6 Do they think she who made the ear is deaf? Or she who fashioned the eye, blind?

7 If entire nations are decimated, how can these fools expect to go unnoticed? Our Mother knows their thoughts and their insipid reasoning.

8 Those who keep your law are the fortunate ones. They will know tranquillity in times of tribulation.

9 In your courthouse a pit is dug for the insidious. But Chokmah will not abandon the sincere or the repentant.

10 The sacred covenant is upheld. The court of justice restores equity and the devoted will follow its rule.

11 I asked, "Who will stand with me against corruption? Who will witness against violent persons?"

12 If Chokmah does not help me, I will be killed. It is only by her faithful love I am held in life.

13 When I am anxious and worried, she comforts me and brings me joy. I know she does not enthrone iniquity.

14 Leaders cause strife when they plot against those dissimilar from themselves. They will not have her protection.

15 Chokmah is my rock, my fortress, and my refuge. She causes evil deeds to recoil on their designers.

16 Chokmah is our judge, our jury, and our witnesses. She prompts corrupt people to self-destruct.

95

1 Sing to Chokmah a joyful song. She is our God, the rock everlasting and our deliverer.

2 Let us come into her presence with gratitude, singing our thanks. Our Great Mother is elemental to all things.

3 Her achievements can be seen in the depths of the earth and on the highest mountains.

4 All hearts and all thoughts are hers, as is the sea and the land. She is the blueprint for everything that is.

5 She is the Mother who has birthed all and she is the substance of all creation.

6 Let us bow down and touch the earth, her body. And let us worship before her.

7 She is our God, our shepherd and our mother. She has carried us safely and warmly within her.

8 She has spoken to us; we heard her words in the quiet places in our hearts.

9 We have not turned away from her nor become stubborn. We have not strayed away for any period of time.

10 Chokmah has vowed, she will not grant the pernicious rest; they will always feel her anger.

96

1 Sing to Shaddai a new song. Sing, all the cosmos, to the Mother.

2 Sing to God, and bless her name! Tell of her protection, given faithfully day after day.

3 Tell stories of her works and tell of the great deeds she has brought into being.

4 Our God, Shaddai, is worthy of praise and she is good beyond all that is.

5 Material possessions, fame, and pleasure are all nothing. Shaddai is the source of delight, gifts, and well-being.

6 Her presence conveys splendor and majesty. In her holy body resides power and beauty.

7 We are the gifts of her body and she feeds us at her breast. Honor the glorious name of Shaddai.

8 Bring your offerings; carry them into her court. Worship Shaddai as is just and befitting.

9 Shaddai is firm and unshakable. She rules hearts with justice and the earth with compassion.

10 She is the bride who comes to give birth. The fields bloom, the seas roar, the trees sing for joy. The earth is glad to be engendered by her.

97

1 Shaddai is everywhere. Let all creation rejoice! Coastal lands rejoice!

2 Clouds and thick darkness gather around her. The only justice is hers and righteousness is the source of her power.

3 Fire precedes her, clearing the way. Lightning illuminates the world; people see her power and tremble.

4 Mountains melt like wax at her sight. The skies display her glory and people know her justice.

5 Those who worship themselves are put to shame. People boasting of worthless deeds are made to feel humiliation.

6 Align your hearts with Shaddai or feel the pain of her rebuke. She is the cosmic Mother and there is no life outside her.

7 She has no evil and those who welcome evil do not walk with her. For she is all wholeness.

8 Her light dawns for the just and illumines their hearts. Rejoice in her and praise her holy name.

98

1 Sing a new song to Shaddai, for she has done marvelous things. Her gentle hands and strong arms have shown her saving power.

2 She has shown mercy and revealed her love to the loyal children. The ends of the earth know her ways.

3 Make happy sounds to praise her. All the cosmos worships her with the song of its being.

4 The melody of life rises to her hearing. The entire body of creation sways in worship of Shaddai.

5 The seas rumble and the fish dance for her. Hills cover themselves in the softness of blossoms to praise her.

6 Reeds sing their thin song and elephants trumpet the fullness of their being for her to hear.

7 The waters of the seashore clap in praise of her works. Joy comes to all beings living in her.

99

1 Shekhinah reigns. All people quiver at her greatness. She sits enthroned with angels and the earth moves with her sways.

2 She stands over her creation and delights in it. Awesome is her being. Praise belongs to her.

3 We bow to you, Chokmah, divine Wisdom. You establish justice and forge honesty. Only one as holy as you can do this.

4 Miriam, Moses, and Jesus invoked her name. They called on Wisdom, and she answered them.

5 Wisdom came clothed in clouds carrying her laws. She teaches us to keep her decrees.

6 Chokmah, divine judge, forgives the penitent and avenges all wrongdoing. Sophia knows all there is to know.

7 Praise the Mother God. Worship at her mountain. She is Chokmah, Sophia, Shekhinah, the holy, powerful, and wise one.

8 Praise the Mother God. Worship at her mountain. She is Chokmah, Sophia, Shekhinah, the holy, powerful, and wise one.

100

1 All creation, make joyous sounds for God. Serve her with gladness.

2 Enter her presence with song. Know Shaddai is our God. She made us and continues to make us.

3 We belong to her. We are her people, the sheep of her pasture.

4 Enter Shaddai's courtyard with thanksgiving and come to her temple with praise.

5 Bless her in the name of Binah, divine womb, seed of holiness. Bless her in the name of Ruach, the wind of life.

6 Give praise to Shekhinah, the God-bride. Bless the name of Chokmah, Divine Wisdom and beginning of all.

7 Indeed, our God is good. She is faithful; her love endures forever and ever.

101

1 I sing to you, O God. The songs of your justice and love give life to me. When shall I be innocent again?

2 I avoid what is base and I hate deceit. I keep my heart open and I practice integrity in my life.

3 I confront those who gossip and I avoid vanity and pride. The arrogant know they have no kinship with me.

4 I seek out loyal friends to share my life with. Those who lead honest lives are welcome to my home.

5 Cheaters and liars are not wanted here. My daily work is to purify the land and beautify the house of Shaddai.

6 I am protector of animals and an advocate for the disadvantaged. Shaddai has charged me to be a patron of her creation.

102

1 Hear my prayer, Shaddai. Let my plea reach you. In my time of need do not turn away from me.

2 In my distress do not hide your face from me. Answer me promptly because my life is passing away like smoke.

3 My bones are brittle, and my arthritis burns as if I am on fire. My skin hangs limpid on my frame.

4 My heart and muscles are worn out like weeds that have lost their fiber. I, who forget to eat, am myself consumed by my grief.

5 All day long I cannot help but groan loudly. At night my eyes are as wide as an owl's in the wilderness.

6 I lie awake, waiting like a solitary bird left on a housetop. And below, my enemies wait for me to fall.

7 My name has become a household curse. No one wants my fate and I am mocked daily.

8 For bread I eat dirt, and my drink is mixed with tears. I was lifted up in anger and thrown aside.

9 My life is now lived in the shadows. I wither in the evening like grass cut in the hot sun.

10 You, Mother, are enthroned forever. Your name endures through all generations.

11 God, you have broken me in my prime, my days are cut short. Do not take me in my half-life, discarded like a torn dress.

12 You will decontaminate the land and return the pride once held by this people. You will rebuild what the pernicious have torn down.

13 You will hear the prayer of the destitute. And these stories will pass on to future generations.

14 In their turn, the unborn will praise you. Prisoners will be granted reprieves and sing to you.

15 Long ago you made the earth and you live on forever. Your years never end.

16 Establish your servant in perpetuity and assure that our children will grow strong in your presence.

103

1 Bless Shekhinah, my soul, with all my being bless her holy name.

2 Bless Shekhinah, my soul, and do not forget her gifts. She forgives all crimes and heals all disease.

3 She saves you from doom; soothes your forehead, calming you. She shows you love and mercy.

4 She satisfies your hunger for security with the comfort of her presence. You grow strong as a young doe with her nurturing.

5 Shekhinah brings justice, defending the oppressed. She teaches her path to those who seek.

6 She is compassionate, tender and caring; slow to anger and quick to love. She has not been as severe to you as you have been with others.

7 Shekhinah's love for those who revere her is as high as the sky. That is how generous she is.

8 She has removed our misdeeds as far as the East is from the West. That is how forgiving she is.

9 Tenderly, as a mother who loves her child is gentle, so is she with her devoted sisters.

10 She knows our weaknesses and our needs. She remembers we are made of earth and we last not much longer than grass.

11 Wind can blow us away, and we are gone, but you, Mother, will last forever.

12 We remember our promise to live as you taught us. Our covenant with you assures the protection of our children.

104

1 Bless Shekhinah, my soul. With all my being bless her holy name. She is clothed in majesty and enrobed in light.

2 The heavens are her home and she rides upon the clouds. She built land over the water and gave it for our abode.

3 The wind delivers her love to us. Her fire warms and thunder wakes us. She is the earth, solid and holding her people securely.

4 The waters obey her and remain within their boundaries. She saves us from death by flooding.

5 Springs gush down mountain ravines, supplying nourishing water for her creatures. Birds and crawling creatures drink side by side.

6 Rain falls on the highlands and fruit grows. She fills the plains with grass for cattle and elephants.

7 She helps people to cultivate the land. She gives us wine to celebrate our joyous events, oil to cleanse our skin, and bread to keep us strong.

8 Cedar, firs, and maples declare her beauty. Birds rest on branches and fill the wind with songs.

9 The moon illumines the darkness and the sun warms the day. She teaches us to balance our life with rest.

10 I will contemplate the majesty of Shekhinah. I will delight in the mystery of her being that is revealed forever.

105

1 Give thanks to Shekhinah, call out her name and tell everyone what she has done. She is strength and constancy.

2 The universe displays her wonders. She does marvelous things for all who are willing to learn.

3 Sarah, Rebecca, Naomi, Leah: all called by her to be her daughters. She chose Joan, Angela, Perpetua, and Hildegard to model courage.

4 She has made a pact with us and we with her. She has called us to be committed and to lead others with wisdom.

5 When the faithful are surrounded by strangers and feel lost, she watches over them as she does for all her children.

6 She protects nuns turned out of their convents during wars. She watches over starving children living in prosperous countries.

7 She punishes governments and rich citizens not caring for the less privileged. Shekhinah remembers their stingy ways.

8 She declares, "Do not harm my chosen sisters, do not hurt my prophets! Feed my children.

9 "I, your Mother, will lead you to the land of fulfillment. Clouds will protect you and fire will enlighten your minds and warm your hearts.

10 "You are mine and everything I have is yours. The oppressive ones will be chased from the land and you will inherit their place."

106

1 Praise Shekhinah for her goodness. Her love endures forever. Her works confound even the most learned.

2 Peace is the gift she gives to the just. She saves us from errors and counts us in her company.

3 We are people capable of iniquity. We are capable of acting badly and we rebel at the notion of forgiving those who harm us.

4 Left to our own devices, we would drown in our discontent. You, Mother, clear away the darkness from our minds and cool our emotions.

5 Weakness and fear are our constant shadows. Rage comes naturally with the experience of desperation, and greed is ever present.

6 You, Ruach, are bigger than life. Your love, Shaddai, is more forgiving than a faithful pet.

7 You are like a tree who gives cover from the burning sun. Your acceptance of differences is encompassing.

8 Mobs kill women healers and those with different beliefs. Prophets, blacks, gays, Indians, all victims of intolerance.

9 We are all endangered by the domination of the insecure and self-righteous. Only when wrapped in her love are we safe.

10 Blessed is the big-breasted Mother, Shaddai, for all eternity. Hallelujah, amen!

107

1 It is right to give thanks to Shaddai. Her goodness endures forever. She rescues us from the darkness of oppression and from our own depression.

2 We are no longer strangers in our own land. We are no longer enemies to ourselves. She teaches us to love and be loved.

3 Hunger and thirst had replaced our courage. We were suffering, and in deep trouble: a wasteland inside, a desert to ourselves.

4 Our hearts were uninhabited and she filled them with love. She satisfied our needs and we hunger no longer.

5 We were humbled; no one knew the true depth of our pain. Now our chains are broken, the darkness lifted, and addictions dispelled.

6 We called out to Shaddai and she heard us; she rescued us from despair. Let us thank Shaddai for breaking down our gates.

7 She healed us when we were overwrought and falling at death's door. Thank Shaddai for the wonders she has worked in us.

8 We were adrift at sea, but she was there. We were staggering on steep cliffs when she held us. We were drunk and she hushed the storms inside.

9 She carried us to a safe cove and held us close to her breast. She turned a desert into lush gardens and fed us.

10 Shaddai has lifted us out of our loneliness and given us a family. We will always rejoice in her ever-present love. Hallelujah!

108

1 My heart is calmed by Shaddai. My spirit is filled with song. I am now awake and see the promise of a new dawn.

2 With my sisters, I will praise what you have done. Your love is more powerful than anything on earth and more vast than the universe.

3 You delivered me and held me close to you. You answered my prayers and protected me.

4 You have brought me into your home. Rejection and self-hatred no longer haunt me. With you at my side I can vanquish any foe.

5 Shaddai has returned my life and my own strength. I am her daughter, mighty and armed against any duress.

109

1 Do not be silent, Chokmah, your wisdom is needed. The enemy has surrounded me and pursues me with their lies.

2 I give support and they denounce me. I adopt their programs and invest in their causes and they attack me.

3 They go before corrupt judges and attempt to entrap others into making statements against me. They will not rest until I am found guilty.

4 They appear to pray but their prayers are really curses. May their careers be cut short; someone else take their jobs.

5 May creditors seize their possessions and no one show them kindness. May their names disappear in one generation.

6 Send their children to far away lands to beg. Let their offspring be orphaned, their spouses bereft, and their families die out.

7 Their parents before them were hard-hearted beasts. May the crimes of their ancestors be held against them.

8 These riffraff never thought of being kind. They cheated the poor and imprisoned the needy. The brokenhearted they hounded to death.

9 They had no desire for blessing others; they never cared for the elderly. Curses came from the depths of their bones, soaking out like oil.

10 Clean suits and smooth faces cannot hide the corruption in their hearts. They pillage anyone not in their own camp.

11 Help me, Chokmah, the world is in need of your wisdom and retribution. The people need your justice.

12 I am an object of derision. People shake their heads when they see me. The world laughs at the stupidity of our nation.

13 Save me because I have loved the people. Day and night, I have worked for the jobless, the disabled, and the youth of our country.

14 Forgive my transgressions and see the goodness in my heart. Give me strength to lead others and remove any shame from my family.

15 My knees are weak, my body gaunt, but you, Chokmah, can restore my position. You will counter their curses with blessings.

16 Deliver me from the bite of these accusers. Cover them in their own iniquity.

17 My errors brought me to you, Chokmah. I bless the opportunity you give me to know hardship and learn from it.

18 I will give thanks to you, Chokmah, for helping the ordinary people and defending them against a sentence of death.

110

1 Chokmah said to me, "Sit at my right hand, until I make your enemies your footstool. I will secure your status and enable you to rule over your enemies."

2 People come freely rejoicing with you on the day of your reprieve. The holy mountains witness the jubilation of the whole country.

3 Youth will flock to you, seeing the chance of a new dawn. Hope will again be as plentiful as dew.

4 Chokmah has sworn and she will not retract. She anointed you to lead. She is at your side.

5 You will shatter the terrorists and judge nations intent on evil. Corpses will cover the land and malicious leaders will be unseated.

6 You will drink from the brook of Chokmah; be strengthened and grow victorious. She will hold your hand, as you support those who need you.

111

1 Hallelujah! Standing in the midst of the just, I praise Chokmah! Your works are great and a wonder for all to behold.

2 Your justice endures secure in strength and clothed with majesty. Surrounding us is the evidence of your wonders.

3 Love and compassion have been reinstated. Food is given to the children. Promises are again sacred.

4 The people know the power of your actions. Truth and fairness are again their legacy and the land and its laws belong to them.

5 Reverence of Chokmah is the beginning of wisdom. Those who have it, display themselves as discerning. Praise to you, Mother, forever.

112

1 Hallelujah! Happiness belongs to those who revere God and delight in her ways.

2 Their children will be blessed and live to govern others. Their households shall be strong.

3 There will be riches and food for their families. For the good of heart, there will always be a light to shine in the darkness.

4 Good people are generous. They lend money without interest. They speak honestly and keep their word.

5 They do not fear bad news. They know justice is immutable and that there is an imperishable memory in the land.

6 They know Shekhinah is merciful, compassionate, and righteous. They know she reveals what lives in the shadows.

7 With peaceful hearts they fear nothing, because their trust is imbedded in our Mother. She and her love are unwavering.

8 They know they will triumph by doing justice and being generous to the poor. Their stores and bank accounts will be replenished.

9 Those who are busy exploiting others will be infuriated when they see this. They will grind their teeth and their hatred will consume them.

10 Finally, the tyrants will vanish like smoke over a dead fire. The just leader, surrounded by her people, will grow stronger each day. Hallelujah!

113

1 Hallelujah! Praise the name of Shekhinah. Bless her name now and forever. Praise her greatness in every place, from the East and to the West.

2 From the rising of the sun to its setting, from the rising of the moon to its setting, bless her holy name.

3 She is above all. She is in all. She is all. Glory to her in the presence of the wonders of her creation.

4 She gives life to everything. She sets the pattern of the seasons. She feeds the hungry. She creates everything out of love and ashes.

5 Shekhinah changes the fortunes of the destitute. Shekhinah gives children to childless mothers. Hallelujah!

114

1 Hallelujah! Shekhinah delivers women from their bondage. She creates families where parents are equals.

2 She sets a balance in relationships. Like the sea, she allows the rhythm of the tide to create a unique equality, nourishing for life.

3 She raises hearts high as mountains and fills them with hope. She plants the grass and gives sweet fruit for strength on the journey.

4 Animals know her and tremble with joy when she approaches. Trees vault forth fruit in recognition of her perfume.

5 The earth quivers like an anxious lover before her beauty revealed. She is the pool of water in which we see our reflection.

6 Springs gush at the touch of her hand. Mother, you melt the hearts of your children and they flow with love for you. Hallelujah!

115

1 Glory does not belong to us, Shaddai. Glory belongs to you for showing us the meaning of faithfulness.

2 Patriarchal nations always parade their gods. They must show their nation's gods are more powerful than another's gods.

3 They buy and sell each other's loyalty. Gold and silver are the standards of success they live by, but never truth.

4 They have mouths but their speech is babble. They have ears but they are deaf. They have eyes but never see beauty or another's need.

5 They have noses but cannot smell their own stench. They have hands but touch no one in tenderness.

6 Their students and supporters are exact copies of themselves. None of them trust each other, yet they always smile.

7 The entourage must parrot the speaker. They are too busy being fearful to ever be happy. These invalids are not capable of praise.

8 We, the children of Shaddai, can live in peace. She has taught us to help the less fortunate. We have no one to fear.

9 We are the children of Shaddai. We love the earth and care for the gifts given to all. We follow our heart's directives.

10 We bless Shaddai forevermore. We are vigorous and will live forever with her. Hallelujah!

116

1 I love you, Shaddai. You have heard my cry and honored my requests. You have turned toward me and touched my face.

2 I was sick and you made me well. I was overcome with worries and you soothed my concerns.

3 You are a gracious and compassionate Mother. You protected the innocent.

4 When I was falling, you caught me. When I needed love, you loved me.

5 My soul can rest in your arms. You are my savior because you have rescued me from death.

6 You have wiped my tears and you have given me a home. You placed me to walk before you like a proud mother.

7 How can I repay you? I will drink a toast to you at every meal. I will tell stories of your love at every gathering.

8 I am alive because of you, Shaddai. I am the child of your fertility, named after you and resembling you. I praise your holy name.

9 In forests and in caverns, I make promises to you. In the clefts of your body, I worship you.

10 In the courtyard of my home you will have an altar. People will know of our love, Shaddai. Hallelujah!

117

1 Praise our God everyone! Sing of her marvels.

2 Her strong embrace will hold us forever.

3 Her love for us is all-powerful.

4 She is faithful forever. Hallelujah!

118

1 Thank you, God. You are good; your love endures forever.

2 When in danger, I call out to Shaddai. She will hear me and ask what she can do for me.

3 Shaddai assures me: "I am with you; fear not. You have the courage to face any consequences. You can fulfill life's demands and learn your strength."

4 God helps me when I feel surrounded. She gives insight to my psyche when it is filled with anxiety.

5 Bees swarm in an intellect that is clouded with self-doubt. Fear, like a sudden brush fire, paralyzes those caught in its grip.

6 Pushed beyond my capabilities, I faint from stress. Shaddai shows me how to see beyond this day.

7 Humbled, I realize my vision is narrow and my heart misled. She shows me I shall not die from this test.

8 Shaddai opens me to know, and I find the right way. She saves me from my own inner blindness.

9 The stone the builders rejected becomes the cornerstone of a solid home. It is the work of Shaddai.

10 Reprieved, I regain my footing and my confidence returns. I bless Shaddai and cover her altar with flowers.

119

1 Happy is the innocent woman. She keeps truth next to her heart.

2 She walks with God and knows inner peace. She honors all persons as divine children.

3 She never dances with evil but keeps her steps guided by principle. She mirrors right behavior and she knows she is blessed.

4 You, daughter of Shaddai, are held closely to the bosom of God. You keep the law and there is no shame in you.

5 Blessed is the woman with an open heart and a clear mind. Truth embeds her in goodness.

6 Her life is filled with beauty and she is confident in herself. Freedom comes to her when truth is acted upon with love.

7 Her heart, inscribed by God, is like a road map to a full life. Prayer opens her mind to honesty and direction.

8 Justice is the destination of the honest woman and truth guides her along the way. Shame and fear have no place here.

9 Riches are found in women who revere God's truths. Shaddai teaches with words that give authentic life.

10 Hope fills my heart because you have touched me with love. Timeless wisdom is the gift she shares with those consoled by her.

11 You, Shaddai, keep your promises. You are the Mother who gives birth to trust.

12 You are the pride beating in my heart, the song rising in my throat. I sleep, folded in the warm garments of your love and consoled by your touches.

120

1 I call out in my anguish and Shaddai hears me.

2 She saves me from conspirators, from their mouths uttering lies.

3 She deals severely with the twisters of truth!

4 Shaddai, the warrior, will save sharp arrows and hot coals just for them.

5 I am an exile in the land of my enemies.

6 I live among those who hate peace.

7 When I speak words of conciliation my enemies reply with acts of war.

121

1 I lift my eyes to the hills and look for help.

2 From their softness, Shaddai will emerge with her strength.

3 She who made all there is will help me.

4 She does not sleep when I call. She steadies my steps.

5 She is my light in darkness and my shade at noon.

6 She hides me from misfortune and saves my soul.

7 Shaddai watches over my comings and goings, now and forever.

122

1 I rejoice when I hear, "Let us go to the house of Shekhinah."

2 Now we are within the protection of the one who contains all.

3 The world is your holy city, built solid. Creation is your temple.

4 We live in you and are nurtured by your milk.

5 It is natural to honor your name.

6 We sit on rock thrones made for us by you.

7 Shekhinah is the rainbow, a pledge of peace.

8 Those who love her find fulfillment and are surrounded by friends.

9 Shekhinah is the midwife of all that is good in us.

10 She makes everything right and keeps us good.

123

1 I raise my eyes to the stars looking for you, Shekhinah.

2 As a devoted friend watches for a sign, or the lover for a smile, I watch for you.

3 I know a favor awaits me, for I am your beloved.

4 I have eaten scorn and have tolerated numerous sneers.

5 The time for enduring mockery and contempt is over.

124

1 If Shekhinah had not heard us and given her protection we would have been lost.

2 Left to ourselves we are chaff consumed in the blazing rage of despots.

3 Evil, like raging water, would have drowned us, swept us away.

4 Blessed be Shekhinah, who did not leave this bird to the teeth of the trap.

5 She gave us strong wings and a flight to freedom.

6 She contains all and is our help in desperate times.

125

1 The woman who trusts in Shekhinah stands solid and firm as Mount Everest.

2 She cannot be shaken; she lives forever. No dominion of wickedness will prevail in her land.

3 Shekhinah is the mountain range protecting her daughters. Her mountains last forever.

4 No autocratic governments can triumph. She gathers the right-hearted and sends the perverse to their doom.

5 Praise be to Shekhinah!

126

1 Even in dreams, our Mother gathers us to her holy mountains.

2 Dancing, songs, and laughter reveal we are restored in spirit.

3 Shekhinah leads us into a new century filled with hope.

4 Wonders await the faithful! A thirst for redemption shall be satisfied.

5 What was sown in anguish will be gathered in joy.

6 Toiling in the garden with tears has made a harvest carried home with song.

127

1 If Shekhinah has not made the world then how do you work in it?

2 If she does not protect and feed you then how do you live?

3 Only the fool thinks anything can be accomplished without her help.

4 Like a vigilant Mother, Shekhinah watches out for her lambs.

5 Even asleep, we are pleasing to her.

6 Children are the glory of those bearing them and we are a blessing to our Mother.

128

1 Happy are you who revere the Mother God and walk in her path.

2 You shall feast on the proceeds of your hard work.

3 Happiness and prosperity are yours.

4 Like cedar shoots, children sprout from the cover of your garments.

5 Your beloved ones grow like a fruitful vine in the warmth of your home.

6 These are the rewards of our loving God.

7 May you live to see your children's children and everlasting peace.

129

1 I have suffered oppression from my childhood but I have never been crushed by it.

2 They scourged my back leaving deep gouges.

3 I was chained and sold as a slave but God set me free.

4 I suffered many deaths, yet lived to watch my enemies die.

5 The winds of Ruach dried them up like grass on a roof, leaving nothing behind.

6 No one blesses the wicked who imprisoned us.

7 No one knows they lived. No worthy deeds survive them.

8 As for us, we are living martyrs bearing children who will tell our stories.

130

1 Out of the depths, I cried to you, O God.

2 Hear my voice; let your ears be attentive to my pleadings.

3 If you, Shaddai, will keep a tally of my sins, how can I stand it?

4 You are forgiving and we are awed by your generosity.

5 With longing, I wait for you and trust in your coming.

6 Dawn comes as surely as you do, Shaddai.

7 Come with your power and rescue me from myself.

8 Free me from the narrowness of my humanity.

131

1 Shaddai, I am not proud nor do I behave with affectation.

2 What is in front of me holds my attention.

3 Like a properly weaned child, I am calm and tranquil.

4 I rest in my Mother's arms sleeping at her breast.

5 My hope is in Shaddai, forever and ever.

132

1 Shaddai, remember Miriam in all her humility.

2 Women in the fields and women washing clothes tell her story.

3 She made a promise that she would not sleep until she had found a home for her people.

4 She carried the Ark and found a safe place to raise children.

5 Now, we sit at her feet and recount what she did. Bravery was her standard.

6 Other women were inspired by her deeds and became leaders.

7 Mary, the mother of Jesus, and Mary the Magdalene gave new hope for salvation.

8 Joan of Arc was anointed by Shaddai to return her people to their homes.

9 We bless our food using their names and remember what they have done.

10 They are your priests, a royal lineage, and we are their children.

133

1 How good and pleasant it is to live like sisters in harmony.

2 It is like receiving a massage with wonderful oil.

3 It is like being clothed in the softest clothes.

4 The dew in the morning and the mist in the hills remind us of this blessing.

5 Shekhinah has begun this work and she continues it, forever and ever.

134

1 Bless Shekhinah, all you who share her gifts.

2 You, who pray through the night and serve her ways, bless her.

3 Lift your arms toward her stars and bless this holy place.

4 May Shekhinah, Mother of the earth, the stars, and the sky, bless you.

135

1 Praise the name of Shekhinah, faithful ones who work in her house.

2 Sing to Shekhinah in her temple courtyard.

3 She chose Mary as her own and blessed her womb.

4 She is greater than all her creation and her will is obeyed.

5 Lightning brings rain and delivers wind from the clefts of her body.

6 She will not stand for injustice and strikes the powerful liars.

7 Shekhinah gives of herself to her daughters.

8 Her name lives forever in the reflections of her beauty.

9 Bless Shekhinah, daughters of Magdalene and women of Esther.

10 Bless her, all you who call her body home. Hallelujah!

136

1 It is good to give thanks to Shaddai. Her love is forever.

2 She alone made the world. Her power is forever.

3 She is the architect of the heavens, her creation is forever.

4 She is the contractor of the land, her steadfastness is forever.

5 She is the seamstress of the night, her stars and moon are forever.

6 She is the fortress of her people, her strength is forever.

7 She is the terror of the wicked, her justice is forever.

8 She is a hero to the brave, her loyalty is forever.

9 She is a mother to the lost, her sweetness is forever.

10 Her bosom comforts and feeds all, her love is forever.

137

1 Alongside rivers we sat weeping, remembering the death of our sisters.

2 In despair, we hung our prayer shawls and musical instruments in trees.

3 Our persecutors shouted for us to dance. How can we dance for the enemy?

4 If the death of our sisters were forgotten, may our hands fall off.

5 If the burning of healers be forgotten, may our voices be silenced.

6 The day they stripped my daughters and smashed them dead with stones will be remembered.

7 Shaddai will never allow these deeds to be forgotten. These crimes will remain always before us.

8 The iniquitous will be paid for their deeds, evil for evil. Doomed are they who killed the women.

9 Their deeds spell out their own demise. And their names will be written and spat on.

10 Their homes will remain empty of love. And any possible children will wither before they are conceived.

138

1 With all that I am, I thank you, Shaddai.

2 In the midst of the chorus of psalmists, I sing to you.

3 I bow toward your holy temple and praise your name.

4 It is by your love and fidelity that all glory is displayed.

5 The distinguished leaders of the world recognize your power.

6 Although you yourself are awesome, you treasure tiny details.

7 Being part of all, you know even the most remote atom.

8 I walk in your hand and I am held safe by your choice.

9 Do not abandon me, the fruit of your womb.

139

1 Mother, you know me as no other can. My secrets are open to you.

2 You follow my coming and my going. My plans are accomplished by your endowment.

3 Before words drop from my lips, your touch silences them. I am struck by your knowledge.

4 If I hide in the deepest cavern, you are there. If I fly to the highest star, you are also there.

5 No darkness is too dark to hide from you; no light too bright to blind you.

6 You wove my inner parts and fashioned me in my mother's womb.

7 You watched my bones assemble and you know the contents of my soul.

8 You watched my body grow according to your design. You recorded my deeds even before I acted.

9 How deep are your thoughts and vast their entirety, numbered more than all the grains of sand lining every shore.

10 You sweep away schemers who malign me. You destroy evil and save me from assassins.

11 You test my deeds and judge my thoughts. You set a fire in my heart.

12 I walk with you, Shaddai, along the path of the ancient sisters. Miriam, Ruth, Sarah—all are one in you.

140

1 Save me, Shaddai, from violent persons. Daily they spawn plots in their hearts.

2 Their evil intentions fly out from lips dripping with venom.

3 Remove me from their reach, free me from their clutch.

4 They continually try to entrap me and thwart my mission.

5 Arrogantly, they pretend to be doing your work. But you see their plan.

6 Shaddai is the fort in which I find safety. She is the helmet that protects me.

7 Do not side with them, Mother. Let them drown in their own venom.

8 Let the impostors stalk each other and drive their own confidants to ruin.

9 Shaddai, throw hot coals on them and toss them into a bottomless pit.

10 As for me, I stand with the innocent. I speak for the voiceless who honor your name.

141

1 I call to you, Mother, come quickly. Hear my pleas and come to me.

2 My prayer rises to you like the smoke of incense. I raise my arms to call you.

3 Set a seal on my lips, O God, and a door around my mouth.

4 Do not allow me to be inclined to speak evil. Never permit me to join the wicked at their wealthy gatherings.

5 If I am reprimanded by the just, help me accept the rebuke with gratitude.

6 The oil of the wicked will never touch me. I will pray against their intrigues.

7 Let them slip off the rock of judgment, pushed off by their own followers.

8 When their bones are broken and they await death, they will call out to you.

9 Shaddai, keep my eyes focused on you. Protect me from unsuspected harm.

10 While these frauds get tangled in their own nets, show me the way to pass free.

142

1 In the depth of my grief, I cry out loud to you, Shaddai.

2 In tears, I pour out the tale of my troubles.

3 I am disheartened and fear my path is full of hidden mines.

4 I am alone and wonder if anyone cares for my friendship.

5 I am trapped and do not know who to turn to for help.

6 I cry to you and realize you are my island of safety.

7 I plead for you to hear me. My strength and pride are gone.

8 I feel hunted and overwhelmed. The power of my conspirators makes me faint.

9 Free me from this cage and set me in the midst of those who love me.

10 Your kindness, Shaddai, will bring me to life. I am humble in the presence of your greatness.

143

1 Shaddai, hear my prayer and listen to my pleading. Answer me.

2 Show compassion and do not judge me harshly. In your presence no one can be found totally innocent.

3 My conspirators stalk me and grind me to dust. They encircle me with the stench of death.

4 My spirit fails and I am frozen in despair. Do not hide from me.

5 I remember when times were better. I remember the wonders of your deeds.

6 I thirst for you in this desert and reach out for your help. Please do not let me die.

7 Stay with me and see me through the night. In the morning I will feel your love and know I am saved.

8 Touch me at your will. I am yours and you are my refuge.

9 Teach me wisdom. Restore my security and satisfy my hunger.

10 Your great love for me disarms my enemies and proves I belong to you.

144

1 Blessed be Shekhinah. She is a warrior who trains me for battle.

2 She is an unfaltering fortress and tower. She is my trusted shield.

3 Shekhinah, why do you worry about people? Humans are like a puff of wind. Their life span is a blink in time.

4 Come, Shekhinah, discharge your arrows at the schemers and scatter them in terror.

5 Lower the clouds, make the mountains smoke, and shoot lightning. Save me from drowning in a sea of deceit.

6 Your power rescues me. I am saved from their razor-sharp tongues.

7 You, Shekhinah, will mold our daughters like the strong pillars that hold up your palace.

8 You bless our fields, fatten our cattle, and fill our pantry with food.

9 Thanks to you, our homes are intact and we have peace in our neighborhoods.

10 We are a blessed people with you as our God.

145

1 I extol my God and my queen. I bless her name forever.

2 Her deeds are honored in stories. Each generation will tell the next one of her greatness.

3 I will reflect on what she has done and sing aloud of her rightness.

4 Shekhinah is slow to anger and quick to love. She is compassionate and loyal to her children.

5 Creation is her continuing glory. Everything happens as she has planned.

6 Shekhinah is gracious to every creature and faithful to every promise.

7 Her gentle touch soothes the forlorn. The entire cosmos suckles at her breast.

8 She holds in her arms those who call her from their hearts. She hears their needs and grants their desires.

9 She gives life to those who love her. All she does is perfect.

10 With all my body, I will sing to Shekhinah. I will bless her forever and ever.

146

1 My spirit sings to God. With all my being I praise Shekhinah.

2 Pretentious people have weaknesses that make them fail. Hope placed in them will not be fruitful.

3 They live for money or looks. There is nothing lasting in them.

4 They are shallow and their deeds crumble into dust. Tomorrow they forget you.

5 Those who are wise hope in God; she knows all hearts. The rules for integrity are set by her standard.

6 She keeps promises forever. She remembers the hungry, the poor, and the imprisoned.

7 She helps the blind see and steadies the feeble. She comforts widows and orphans.

8 She protects strangers and shields those seen as different. She clears the minds of the confused.

9 Shekhinah assists good people and sets barriers in the path of the wicked.

10 Shekhinah continues through generations. Children, praise her name. Hallelujah!

147

1 How good it is to sing to God. How marvelous is the sound.

2 Shekhinah remakes the world and gathers together wounded warriors.

3 She heals broken bodies and revives saddened spirits. She knows the stars by name.

4 She feeds the ravens when they call. She holds the net that catches the good and she allows the wicked to fall through.

5 Sing a song of thanksgiving to her. Play music for her pleasure.

6 She delights in the strength of a horse and the swiftness of an athlete.

7 She favors the kind and loves the faithful. She smiles at the respectful.

8 She guards the pregnant and fills their homes with grain. Peace is her gift to the fertile.

9 When she speaks the cosmos hears; winds blow, ice melts, and streams flow.

10 To Naomi, and others whose names are not recorded, she gave her wisdom. Hallelujah!

148

1 Praise Shekhinah, from the highest heavens. Praise her, all angels.

2 Praise her, sun and moon. Praise her, glittering stars.

3 Praise her, waters below the clouds and waters under the earth.

4 For she has set you in place and holds you there.

5 Praise Shekhinah, all variations of creation. She has created your diversity.

6 Fire, hail, snow, and wind obey her voice. Mountains, cedars, wild animals sing her praise.

7 Nobility and common people, leaders and workers, children and the elderly praise her.

8 Her name is greater than all others. Her glory is displayed in the heavens.

9 She has anointed us with pride and crowned us with her heritage.

10 Shekhinah has held her creatures close to her. Praise her holy name.

149

1 Sing to Shekhinah a new song in a new century. Let all creation rejoice in their Mother.

2 Dance in her name a new dance, one that reveres all her procreation, all her motherly fecundity.

3 Shekhinah balances all debts. She delights in saving every helpless person.

4 Now, she gathers her daughters for a ritual, a new sacrament. But one that was begun prior to the days of Ishtar.

5 Let praise for Shekhinah be on their lips and a sword be in their hands to reclaim their heritage.

6 It is time to punish the irreverent. It is time to discipline the destructive and regain women's rightful place.

7 It is time to jail the polluters and put oppressors in chains. It is time to complete a circle almost broken.

8 It is time for women to repossess the honor taken away by patriarchal leaders. Their lust for power and violence forbade the honor of women.

9 Justice demands that they have every opportunity to change. Now their time of dominion has ended.

10 The accomplishment of God's justice is the glory of the faithful. Hallelujah!

150

1 Hallelujah!

2 Praise! Praise Shekhinah in her holy temple. Praise her in the highest heavens.

3 Praise! Praise Shekhinah with trumpet fanfare. Praise her mighty deeds and her nobility.

4 Praise! Praise Shekhinah with drums and flutes. Praise her on the harp and violin.

5 Praise! Praise Shekhinah with crashing cymbals and ringing bells. Praise her with dances and the melody of chant.

6 Praise! Praise Shekhinah with the warmth of the earth and the softness of the sea. Praise her with the moist breath of every living thing.

7 Praise! Praise Shekhinah and sing Hallelujah!

8 Praise! Praise Shekhinah and sing Hallelujah!

Bibliography

Andrew Harvey and Anne Baring, eds., *The Divine Feminine: Exploring the Feminine Face of God Throughout the World* (Berkeley, CA, 1996).

Elizabeth A. Johnson, *She Who Is: The Mystery of God in Feminist Theological Discourse* (New York, 1992).

Daniel C. Matt, *The Essential Kabbalah: The Heart of Jewish Mysticism* (San Francisco, CA, 1995).

Judith Plaskow, *Standing Again at Sinai: Judaism from a Feminist Perspective* (New York, 1990).

www.northcoast.com Mystic Judaism And The Ten Sefirot (Peter and Gretchen Schutz, University of California, Davis)

www.hjem.get2net.dk/333/qabalah Copenhagen Qabalah

www.argotique.com/qabalah Argotique – The Tree Of Life –

www.faithfutures.org/Bible/sophia Wisdom/Sophia texts in the Old Testament

www.northernway.org Sophia, Goddess of the Hebrew Bible and New Testament

www.inner.org The Sefirot

www.ucalgary.ca Sefirot